Basic Rug Hooking

Basic Rug Hooking

Complete Guide to Tools and Materials
Step-by-step Instructions and Photos • 5 Beginner Projects

Edited by Judy P. Sopronyi

Consultant editor
Janet Stanley Reid

Photographs by
Alan Wycheck

STACKPOLE
BOOKS
Guilford, Connecticut

STACKPOLE BOOKS

An imprint of Globe Pequot, the trade division
of The Rowman & Littlefield Publishing Group, Inc.
4501 Forbes Blvd., Ste. 200
Lanham, MD 20706
www.rowman.com

Distributed by NATIONAL BOOK NETWORK

British Library Cataloguing in Publication Information available

Library of Congress Cataloging-in-Publication Data Is Available

ISBN: 978-0-8117-7054-5 (pbk. : alk. paper)   **33614082452359**
ISBN: 978-0-8117-7055-2 (electronic)

♾™ The paper used in this publication meets the minimum requirements of American National Standard for Information Sciences—Permanence of Paper for Printed Library Materials, ANSI/NISO Z39.48-1992.

Contents

Acknowledgments

Thanks to Janet Stanley Reid for her rug hooking expertise, guidance, enthusiasm, and willingness to do whatever was necessary to help bring this book to rug hooking newcomers. As I worked with Janet on this book, I often thought of my late mother, Lorrene Mae (Moore) Patterson, who shared with me her love of working with textiles.

Introduction

Janet Stanley Reid, a rug hooker with eighteen years of experience, loves to teach beginners. In this book, she shares her knowledge of the craft and her teaching experience to take you step by step through the process, with lots of tips to help you develop and refine your skills.

Spend some time with chapters 1 and 2 to get an understanding of rug hooking tools and materials and some familiarity with the basic motions involved in rug hooking. For the most part, the later chapters progress from simple to more difficult projects, with new skills and techniques introduced along the way.

Once you're comfortable with the process, give some thought to developing your own patterns. That's the way the craft started out, and we encourage you to carry that history forward.

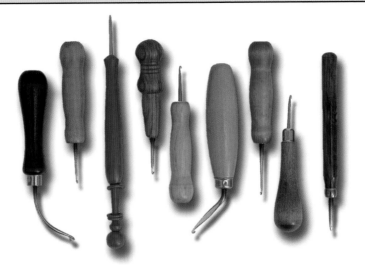

Part I

Basic Tools and Skills

1

Tools and Materials

There are many tools and materials available that add to the ease of rug hooking. However, keep in mind that the craft began with some imagination, a bent nail, a burlap feed bag, a pair of scissors, and the good parts of worn-out clothing. While we highly recommend that you scrap the idea of a bent nail and buy a hook, there are alternatives to high-priced gizmos.

When you're just starting out, you might want to try some of the simpler tools before you launch into the purchase of such things as hooking frames and cutters.

Refer to the resources in the back of the book for companies that provide the more specialized rug hooking tools and materials.

Wool

Quality counts with the wool you select. The ideal weight is 12 to 14 ounces per yard. If you're uncertain of the weight, cut a piece 36 x 36 inches and weigh it on a postal or kitchen scale. The Dorr Mill Store, Woolrich, and the Wool Studio specialize in fabrics for rug hooking, as do rug hooking shops.

Blends of wool and man-made fibers such as polyester do not tear as well as 100 percent wool. Tearing determines the lengthwise or crosswise grain of the fabric prior to cutting.

By cutting strips from the different color areas of plaids, you'll have hues that you can rely on to work well together.

The wool needs to be fairly tightly woven, or the strips you cut will simply separate into individual threads. This example (above) is too loosely woven for hooking strips, but it could be used as a backing.

Visit thrift shops to find clothing made of attractive wool, but keep in mind that the finish of worsted wool such as in men's suits is too flat, and the wool of a winter coat is too heavy. Thrift shop kilts and fabric from a pair of pants yield plenty of desirable, inexpensive wool.

Backings and Hooks

The foundation of your work should be of good quality. Hooked rugs can last for generations, so an investment in a good backing is well worth it. Buy backing from a rug hooking source to be sure you're getting the quality you need.

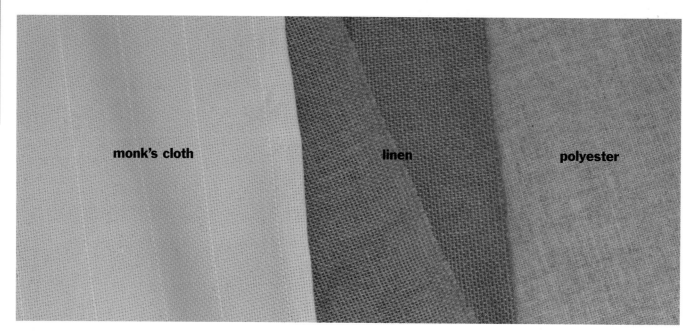

monk's cloth linen polyester

MONK'S CLOTH

Although you can buy this even-weave cotton backing in fabric shops, the weight and strength may not be appropriate. The monk's cloth available from hooking shops has a lighter-colored thread incorporated in the weave to aid in keeping patterns straight.

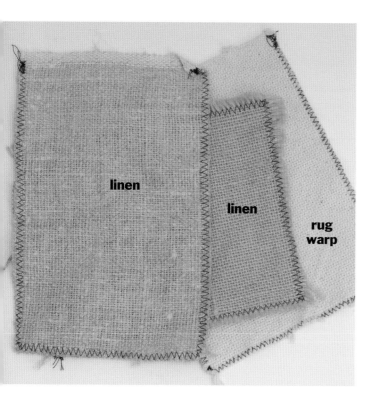

linen linen rug warp

LINEN

This strong, durable fabric is ideal for rug hooking. Buy the type available from hooking resources to be assured of the appropriate weight and density. The color is usually unbleached and neutral. It's available in a smooth, "hairless" version as well as a rougher type.

POLYESTER

This is a fairly new material available for rug hooking. It comes in several colors such as oatmeal, soft blue, and rose, which make it especially desirable for projects such as *Red* in chapter 3 where the background is left unhooked. It's also called Verel or panel fabric, owing to its use on cubicle dividers in offices.

RUG WARP

Rug warp is cotton and similar to monk's cloth. The threads in the fabric are heavier than in monk's cloth, and whereas monk's cloth has two threads woven together, rug warp has one. Rug warp is especially good for larger rugs. It's shown at left lying beneath two varieties of linen backing.

BURLAP

Originally used as a backing when the craft of rug hooking developed, burlap has been found not to wear well and is not recommended for modern rugs. Burlap is made of jute with short fibers that don't interlock. The weave loosens when damp and contracts when dry, resulting in quick wearing and broken fibers.

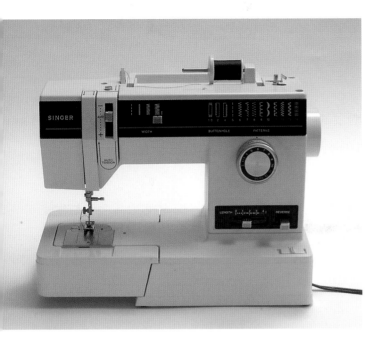

MASKING TAPE

This is another way to keep the edges of backing fabric from fraying. Just fold it over the edge lengthwise.

SEWING MACHINE

While not necessary, a zigzag-equipped sewing machine can quickly protect the raw edges of the rug backing. Use the zigzag stitch to sew along the raw edges to keep them from fraying. The straight stitch of a sewing machine is also used for attaching the binding in chapter 4, although the binding can be sewn on by hand.

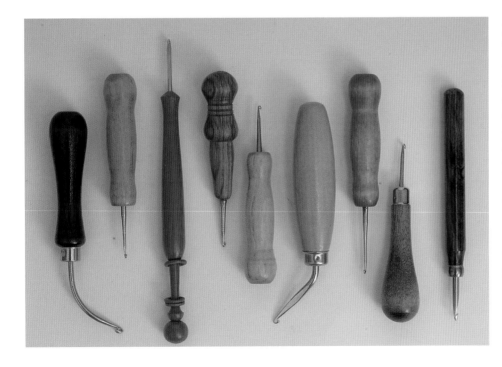

HOOKS

This necessary tool pulls strips of wool from beneath the backing to form loops. Many different handle styles are available. Choose one that feels good in your hand. Hooks also come with a wider shank to aid in enlarging holes for wider wool strips, and some shanks are bent, which you may find more comfortable to use. Size medium or coarse hooks work well for strip width cut sizes #5 and up. For narrow cuts such #3 or #4, look for a fine hook, marked "F" on the end of the handle. (Page 11 shows cut sizes.)

Transfer Aids

There are several ways to copy a pattern onto a backing.

PINS

Quilting pins work well for holding patterns in place and for use in finishing bindings and cording. Smaller dressmaker pins can also be used.

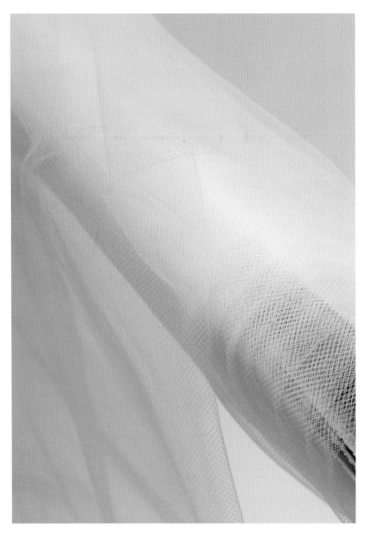

TULLE

This fine, transparent fabric associated with bridal veils can be used to transfer patterns from paper to backing. Just pin the tulle to the pattern, trace it with a marker, pin the traced tulle to the backing, and trace again.

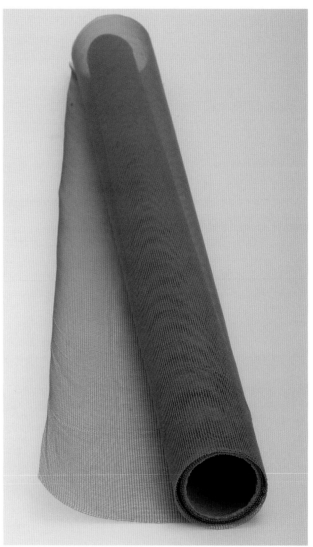

SCREENING

Gray (not black) window screening can also be used to transfer patterns from paper to backing. It's less stretchy than tulle, but the traced pattern is harder to see on the screening than on tulle.

MEASURES

Use rulers, yardsticks, and tape measures to measure the outer border of the pattern on the backing and to measure wool.

PENCIL

Use a pencil with relatively soft lead to mark the outer dimensions of a pattern on backing fabric, letting the pencil trail between threads along the grain of the backing fabric.

TRANSFER PENCIL

Transfer designs with this iron-on transfer pencil. Instructions are included on the packaging.

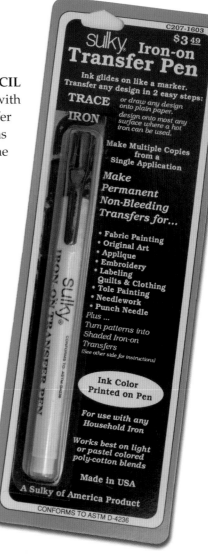

PERMANENT MARKERS

Use a black permanent marker, such as a fine-point Sharpie, to trace designs from paper patterns onto tulle or window screening and then onto the backing. Use a different color to make alterations to a design.

Frames

A frame holds the backing for a hooked rug taut so that loops of wool can easily be pulled through the backing. Until you know that you want to continue with the craft of rug hooking, you might want to start with an old picture frame, canvas stretchers, or a quilting hoop, before you invest in a rug hooking frame. Frames designed specifically for rug hooking raise the work so it's easier to hold wool strips beneath it. They also have gripper strips that make it simple to stretch the backing on the frame, lift it off, and reposition it.

Prices for hooking frames range from about $50 to $500, though you can often find bargains on the leading internet auction sites such as Ebay.

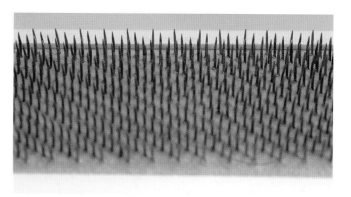

Frames designed for hooking have tiny, needlelike projections along each side, called gripper strips. The strips are ideal for holding the backing taut and for easily repositioning the backing for larger hooked pieces.

PICTURE FRAMES

A sturdy picture frame can be used as a hooking frame. Use upholstery tacks to hold the backing in place.

CANVAS STRETCHERS

Artists' canvas stretchers come in many lengths and can serve as a hooking frame, along with upholstery tacks to secure the backing. They're sold at craft and art supply shops.

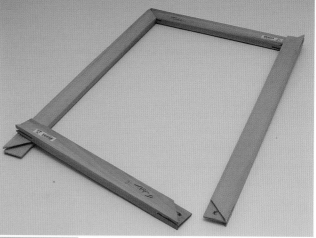

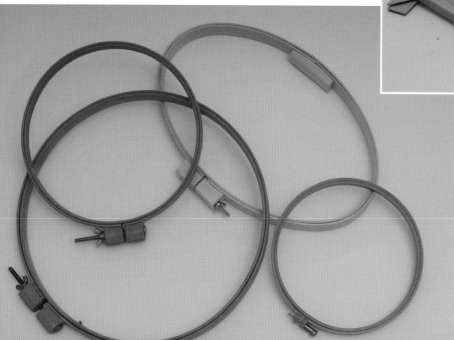

QUILTING HOOPS

The different sizes and shapes of quilting hoops make them useful as hooking frames for beginners. They're fine for smaller projects where the hooking will fit entirely within the hoop. The hoops tend to crush the wool loops of larger projects.

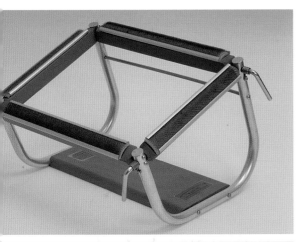

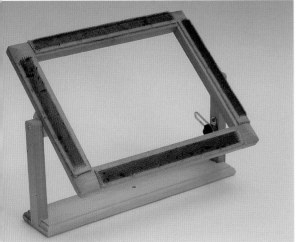

STANDING FRAMES

This standing frame can be adjusted for tilt. It's meant to be pulled up to a chair. The large frame makes it possible to work a bigger rug without having to frequently reposition it.

LAP FRAMES

Lap frames, as their name suggests, rest on the hooker's lap and leave room for one hand to work beneath the frame. The angle of the metal lap frame is set, while the angle of the wooden one varies in response to light pressure. The metal frame pictured has levers at the upper and lower right to aid in tightening the backing.

STANDS

Stands are available that accommodate a lap frame and also have a small platform for a cutting machine. This platform has holes for scissors, too. Height is adjustable.

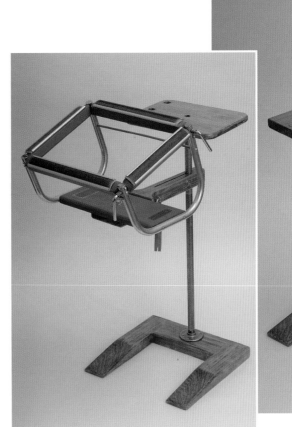

9

Cutters

Before you buy a cutter, try cutting by hand with a pair of scissors. It won't take much hand-cutting for a small project such as *Red* in chapter 3. Some people enjoy the scissors work, and it doesn't have to be done all at once. If you dislike hand-cutting or want to do a lot of hooking, consider one of these cutting machines. Each has a hand crank to feed the fabric through the cutter head. Start out with something basic like the Bliss or the Fraser 500. Later you can move up to something like the Bolivar or Bee Line Townsend and keep your first cutter set to cut strip widths you use less frequently.

Prices range from about $50 to $500, which includes at least one cutter head, but you can often find a strip cutter for less on one of the popular internet auction sites such as Ebay.

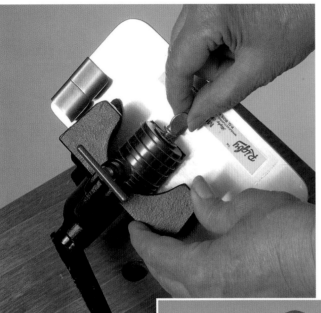

FRASER 500
This basic strip cutter has interchangeable heads for cutting different strip widths.

RIGBY
The Rigby has two cutter heads and is also available with a single cutter head. Interchangeable cutter heads are available. A thumb screw holds the head in place.

BOLIVAR
This cutter has three cutter heads attached that can be rotated into position for quick changes for different strip widths.

BLISS
The Bliss Portable Strip Slitter has interchangeable cutter heads for different strip widths. Unlike the other cutters shown here, the Bliss does not have a clamp to secure it to a surface but instead has gripper feet.

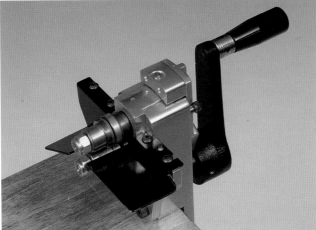

BEE LINE TOWNSEND

The cutter heads drop into the top of this machine for easy size changes. Each drop-in cuts one size.

CUTTER HEADS

The sharp, grooved edges of these heads cut wool fabric into strips, with the narrower grooves cutting narrower strips. Bliss and Fraser machines use the same cutter heads. The heads cost about $15 each.

CUT STRIP WIDTHS

Rug hooking instructions refer to strip widths by "cut" number. The cut number is based, for the most part, on 32nds of an inch, so #8 cut is $8/32$ inch or $1/4$ inch.

Here are strips of different cut widths, shown actual size. Each is labeled by its cut number. The size in inches is shown in parentheses.

#3 ($3/32$ inch)

#4 ($1/8$ inch)

#5 ($5/32$ inch)

#6 ($3/16$ inch)

#7 ($7/32$ inch)

#8 ($1/4$ inch)

#8 $1/2$ ($5/16$ inch) (#10 for the Bolivar cutter)

#9 ($3/8$ inch) (#12 for the Bolivar cutter)

SCISSORS

Dressmaker shears are useful for cutting wool, tulle, backing fabric, cord, binding tape, yarn, and thread, while smaller scissors are better for trimming strip ends. Bent scissors such as those used for appliqué work well for this. Choose scissors with comfortable handles.

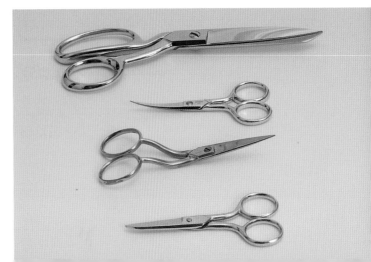

Binding

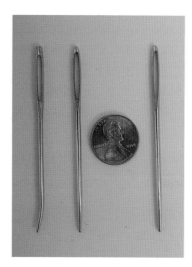

NEEDLES

Large tapestry needles or yarn needles are used for whipping yarn around rug edges. Some rug hookers find that a needle with a bent tip is more convenient to use.

Needles for whipping down the edges of rug binding tape need to have an eye big enough to accommodate the thicker thread being used and a strong enough shank to pierce the hooked backing without bending, such as the one shown at left.

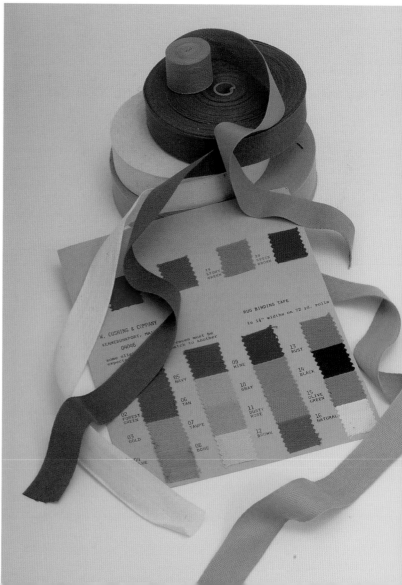

RUG BINDING TAPE

These cotton tapes are 1 $1/4$ inches wide and come in many colors.

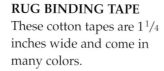

YARN

Yarn for whipping the corded edges of rugs should be wool and in a color that closely matches the background of the rug. Merino works well.

PLIERS

Use pliers to help in pushing and pulling a needle through the piping along the edge of a rug. Regular needle-nose pliers will work. Shown here are bent-tip pliers that provide a more convenient angle.

CORD (PIPING)

The $1/4$-inch cord used for finishing the edges of the rug should be of cotton.

THREAD

For whipping binding tape to the back of the rug, use a strong thread such as buttonhole twist or quilting thread. Choose polyester, cotton, or a blend of the two.

13

Steaming

TOWELS
Old towels, wet and wrung out, are placed above and below a hooked piece when steaming it.

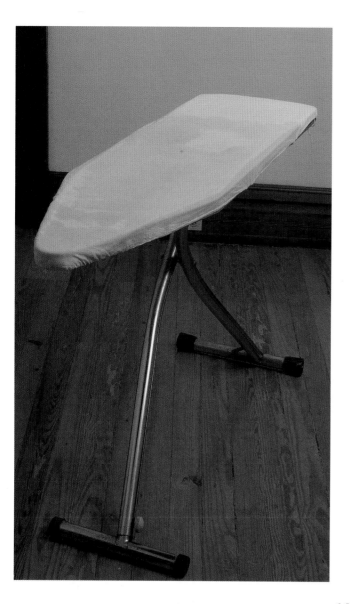

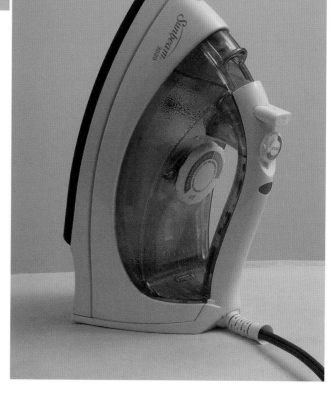

IRON
An iron is necessary for steaming a finished rug. It needn't be a steam iron, as all the steam comes from wet towels placed above and below the hooked piece.

IRONING BOARD
An ironing board provides a sturdy surface for steaming a rug, although some people protect a table or other waterproof surface with lots of padding and use it for steaming.

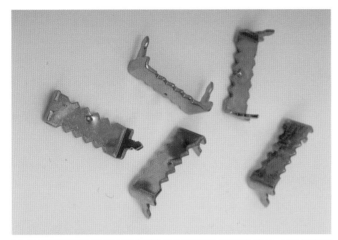

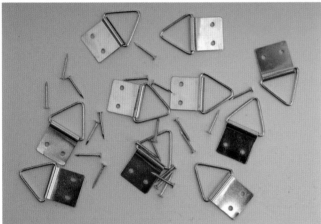

HANGING HARDWARE
Several varieties of hanging hardware can be tacked to a wooden support on the back of a rug for hanging.

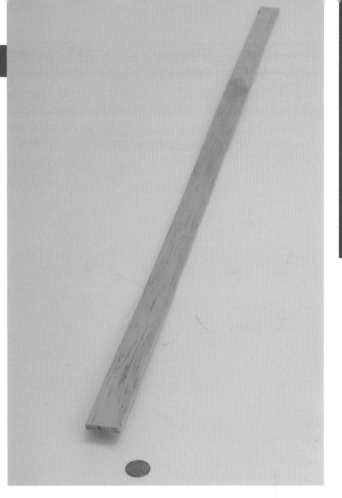

LATH
A wooden lath from a hardware store, slipped into a narrow sleeve of fabric called a casing sewn along the back top edge of a rug, will support it for hanging. It's the size used in wooden lattice.

FURNITURE WEBBING
This webbing, folded in half lengthwise and sewn together on the long edge, makes a good casing or sleeve for a strip of wooden lath to support a hanging rug. It's sold at fabric, craft, and upholstery shops.

Pedula Flowers

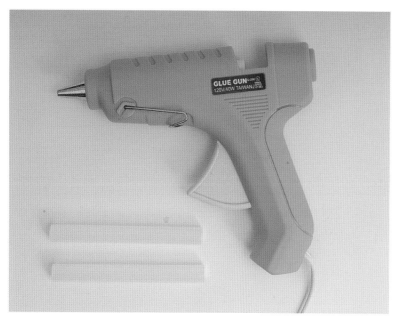

GLUE GUN AND GLUE STICKS
Assemble the pedula flower pins with quick-drying hot glue.

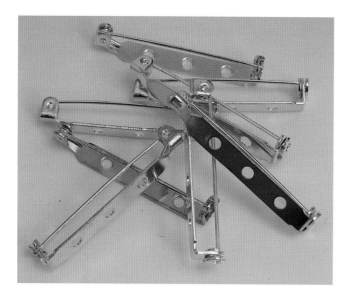

PIN BACKS
Glue or sew these to the backs of pedula flowers to transform them into wearable art.

GLUE
Aleene's Tacky Glue makes quick work of finishing the edges of the pedula flowers in chapter 7.

2

How to Hook

Rug hooking is a simple process, involving piercing a piece of rug backing with a hook, catching a strip of wool fabric with the hook, and pulling a loop of the wool to the front of the backing. We show you how it's done using regular rug backing of monk's cloth and also with a wide mesh so you can see what's happening on both sides of the backing.

All the instructions in this book show the process right-handed. If you're left-handed, you might want to try hooking right-handed, or just reverse the directions.

To avoid confusion, some of the following photos are labeled "above" and "below." The "above" photos show the right hand working on the top or front of the backing. The "below" photos show the left hand working on the underside of the backing. The wide-mesh photos all show the hooking process from above.

TOOLS AND MATERIALS

Monk's cloth, linen, or polyester backing: large enough to fit on a rug hooking frame or a sturdy quilting hoop

Rug hooking frame or quilting hoop

Wool fabric: approx. 1 x 14 inches

Dressmaker shears

Hook: medium or coarse

Small scissors

1. Stretch the backing from top to bottom and, holding it taut, place it on the hooking frame or quilting hoop.

If you are using a picture frame or a frame of canvas stretchers, lay the backing over the frame with the threads of the backing (the grain) lined up with the top, bottom, and sides of the frame. Insert an upholstery tack through the backing into the frame at the top center. Gently stretch the backing down from the tack to the bottom center and insert another tack at the bottom center. Working from the center tacks to each side, insert another tack every inch or so, gently stretching the backing to keep it taut and straight on the frame. Tack the sides the same way.

For a quilting hoop, first remove the inner hoop ring from the outer ring. Push the outer ring down over the backing and inner ring. If the backing seems too slack in the frame, tug the loose outside edges until the backing is evenly taut and the backing threads (the grain) are straight and not wavy. If the outer loop seems loose and won't hold the backing taut, tighten the wing nut on the outside edge of the hoop.

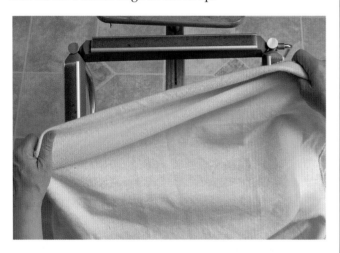

2. Grip the sides of the backing, lift slightly, stretch them taut, and resettle the sides of the backing on the frame. The backing should be smooth, straight, and taut on the frame.

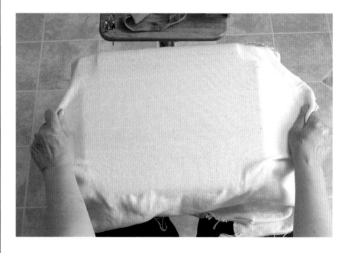

3. Always tear the wool lengthwise first to be sure you have a straight edge. Measure $1/2$ inch from the torn edge of the wool fabric. Insert a pin at the $1/2$-inch mark, parallel with the torn edge.

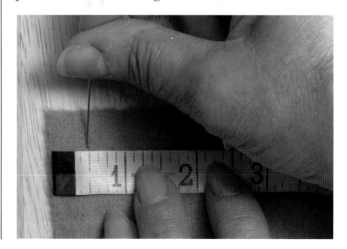

4. Use scissors to clip the wool alongside the pin, from the edge to the pin and parallel to the torn edge.

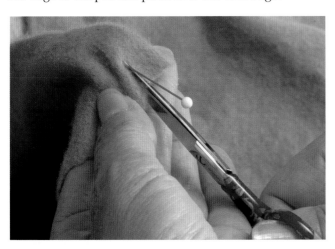

5. Beginning where you clipped, tear a ¹/₂-inch-wide strip of wool. Woven wool fabric tears straight, so the torn strip will be a uniform ¹/₂-inch width its entire length. Loosely woven wools and wools mixed with man-made fibers do not tear easily and should be avoided.

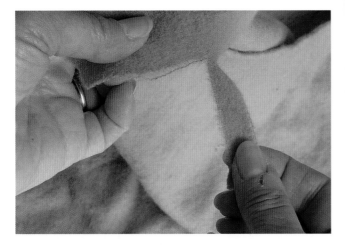

6. Cut the ¹/₂-inch strip lengthwise down the center with scissors to create two ¹/₄-inch strips.

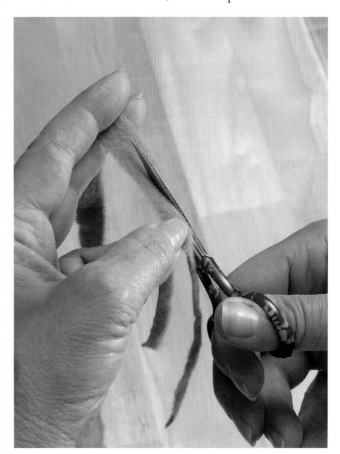

7. Hold the strip of wool with your left hand, under the portion of the backing where you want to start. Here the strip is held with one end between the first and second fingers and the other between the thumb and third finger. (Some people simply hold the strip between their thumb and index fingers with an inch or so of the short end of the strip sticking up.)

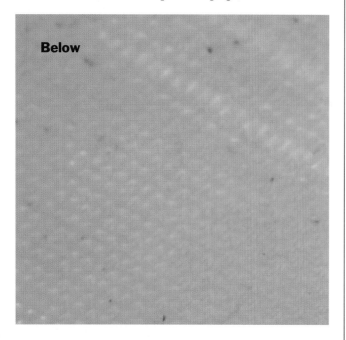

Below

8. Holding the hook comfortably in your right hand (there is no correct or incorrect way to hold it), turn it so that the hook is toward your left thumb.

Above

Pierce a hole in the backing (a space between threads of the backing) with the hook.

Above

The mesh shows the position of both hands as the hook pierces the backing to pull up the end of the wool strip below.

9. Under the backing, catch the strip with the hook. With your thumb, lay the strip against the hook shaft with the bottom of the strip resting in the hook.

10. Use the hook to pull the end of the strip up through the backing. Be sure to catch the entire width of the strip so that you don't separate it with your hook. You may need to practice a few times until you can grab the entire width. Hook the strip at least 1 inch from its end.

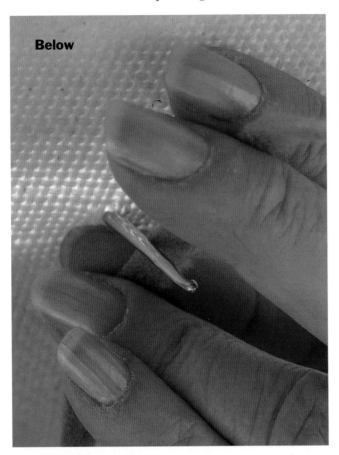

Below

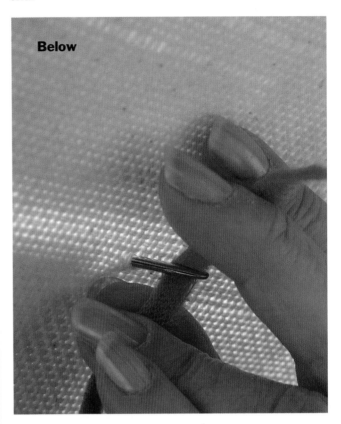

Below

Below

21

Below

The hook pulls the end of the strip up through the backing.

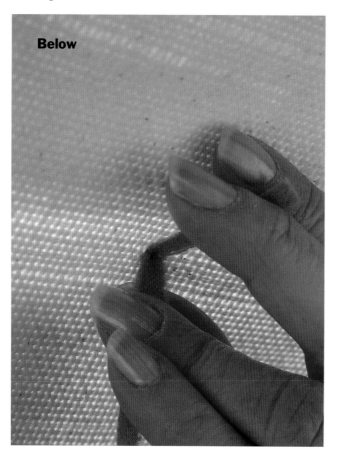

Below

The strip is pulled to the front of the backing. It will appear first as a loop until the shorter end of the strip comes all the way out of the backing.

Above

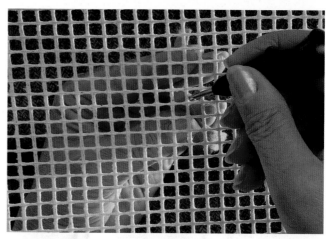

11. When you pull up the loop, release the short end with your left hand so you can pull the strip end through the backing with the hook. Leave the end of the strip as it is, sticking up through the backing.

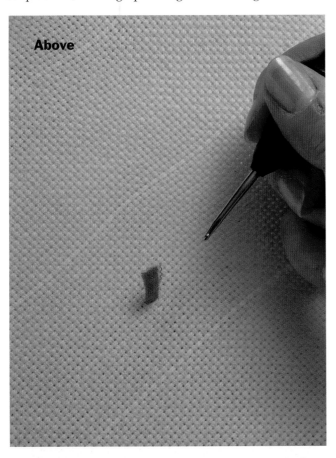

Above

12. Hold the long end of the strip under the backing with your left thumb and index finger.

Below

13. Use the hook in your right hand to pierce the backing through the hole next to the strip you pulled up.

14. Pull up a loop of wool. The loop should be as high as it is wide. Since the strip is ¼ inch wide, pull up a ¼-inch-high loop.

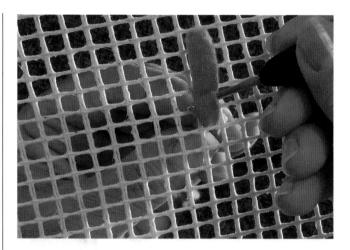

Above

15. With the loop still on the hook, "lean" it back against the strip you pulled up before. This will help keep the loop from being pulled out when you pull up your next loop.

16. Continue pulling up loops, leaning each one back against the preceding loop, until you feel comfortable with the process. As you hook each loop, make sure it is the same height as the preceding loop. If a loop is too high, tug the strip end under the backing. If a loop is too short, pull it higher with the hook. If you notice that a loop farther back in a series of loops is too long or short, don't try to adjust it by pulling from below the backing. Instead, pull the end of the strip from under the backing to remove all the loops hooked after the problem loop. (See step 20.) Then adjust the problem loop as above and continue hooking from there.

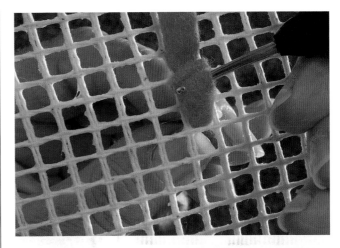

17. Check the height of your loops by holding a ¹/₄-inch strip of wool beside them. Whichever size of strip width you're using, the loops should be as tall as the strip is wide, unless you're using two different strip widths for the same project. In that case, the rule of thumb is to hook loops as high as the width of the widest strip.

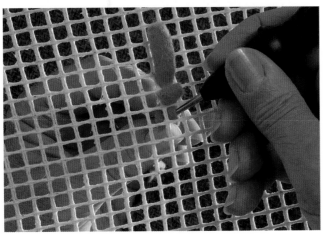

18. With a ¼-inch strip, hooking in every hole will make your hooking too tight. Skip a hole now and then. This example shows hooking that is too tightly spaced. The crowded loops make the backing bulge up, and no amount of steaming will flatten it.

19. Hook another row beside the first row you hooked. The edges of the loops should "touch shoulders" snugly but not tightly. The snugness helps hold the loops in place.

Here's an example of loop rows that are too far apart. On the front, the backing will show through the loops, especially over time as the piece wears.

This example shows what correct spacing looks like on the back of a completed rug. Not much of the backing shows.

20. Errors are easy to correct. Simply pull the wool strip from under the backing.

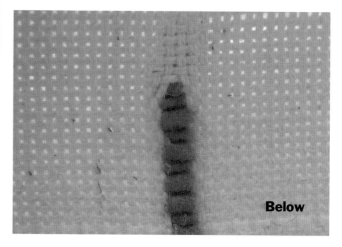

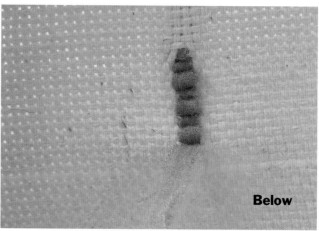

The strip pulls out effortlessly from the back.

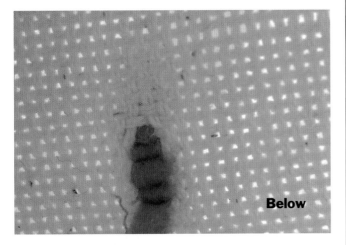

Below

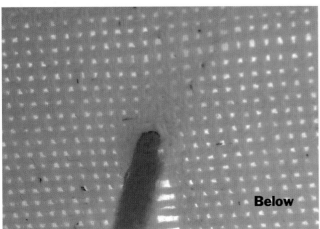

Below

The removed strip will leave spaces where the loops were.

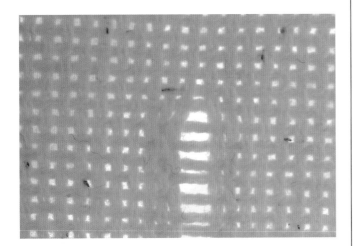

Use your fingernail to scratch the threads of the backing together as they were before.

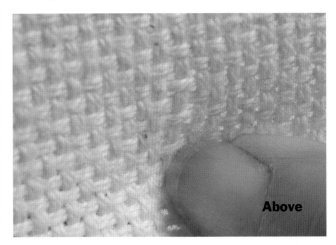

Above

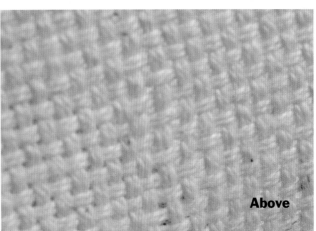

Above

21. The ends of strips are always on the top of the backing, never on the bottom. When you run out of strip, pull the end to the top.

22. In the same hole through which you pulled the end to the top, pull up the end of the new strip. Two colors are used here so you can clearly see where one strip ends and the next begins.

23. Then begin pulling up loops.

After you've hooked a few loops past the place where you started the new strip, snip off the tops of the strip ends level with the tops of the loops.

The two cut strip ends blend in and almost disappear.

Here's an example of a gold strip going across the back instead of being brought to the top and clipped. The strip could easily snag—pulling all the loops out with it—and quickly wear out.

Outlining each shape before it is filled in is a good practice and gives a crisp shape to the motifs. This is one of the reasons why many of the directions in this book say "outline and fill." It is important to keep your hooking within the lines of the pattern to keep shapes from ballooning out of proportion. An exception is hooking a single row as for a stem, where you should hook directly on the pattern line.

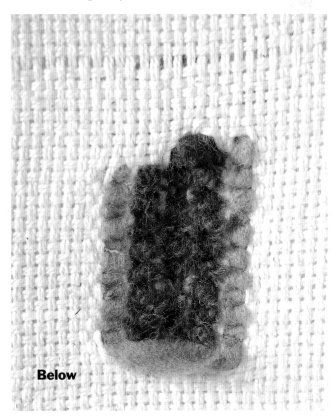

Below

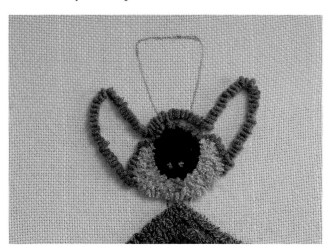

Avoid having several strip ends in a row, as in the example where a row of gold strip ends lines up alongside the row of rust. Hooking up to the rust and then continuing with the gold in the opposite direction, without starting and stopping with cut gold ends, will give a more pleasing appearance.

The projects on the following pages will help you develop your skills and knowledge. For the most part, they progress from simple to more difficult, except for chapter 7, which has an easy, quick project.

Part II

Projects

3

Red for Framing

Picture frame by Rebecca Erb.

Janet Reid's sprightly barnyard critter is a perfect first project because the rooster is small—the framed area is only 8 x 10 inches. You could use a large embroidery hoop instead of a hooking frame. Most of the loops are a wide #8 cut ($^1/_4$ inch), so the hooking goes quickly. To make things even simpler, the background is left unhooked. Here the design is shown hooked on a polyester backing called Verel.

Red would be right at home hanging on a wall near a breakfast table or in the kitchen. He'd also make a dandy pillow top.

RED

**Pattern shown actual size,
8 x 10 inches**

Pencil

Ruler

Polyester backing: 16 x 18 inches
(large enough to fit on the hoop or
hooking frame you're using)

Bridal tulle: 10 x 12 inches

Quilter or dressmaker pins

Permanent marker, black

Sewing machine with zigzag (optional)
and thread

Masking tape (optional)

Wool fabric*
(swatches on page 35)

Gold check (wing):
1 x 29 inches (1 strip)

Red plaid (body): 1 x 29 inches

Solid gold (eye, legs, beak, tail):
1 x 29 inches

Rust (tail, comb, wattle):
1 x 29 inches

*The wool fabric doesn't need to be 29
inches long. It could also be 2 x 14½
inches or another dimension, as long
as you have about 29 square inches
(1 x 29 = 29; 2 x 14½ = 29).*

Dressmaker shears

Cutting machine with #8 and #4 cutting wheels
(optional)

Hook: medium

Embroidery or quilting hoop or hooking frame:
10 x 10 inches minimum

Small scissors

Ironing board and iron

Old towel

Red for Framing

1. Leaving a 4- to 5-inch border all around (or large enough for this small piece to fit on your hooking frame, if you're using one), use a pencil and ruler to draw the 8 x 10-inch outline of the pattern onto the backing fabric. Be careful to draw along the lengthwise and crosswise grain (the direction of the fibers) of the fabric. Backings for rug hooking have prominent grain, and some, such as monk's cloth, have lines woven in to facilitate keeping the pattern straight on the backing. You should be able to easily trail the pencil tip along the grain of fabric (in the "trench" between threads) without having to use a straight edge for help. The ruler is only for measuring.

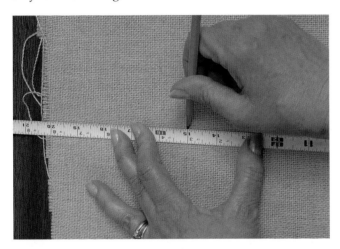

Wool colors

We used an autumnlike palette of rusty reds and golds for this rooster. If you'd like to try different colors, see chapter 4, page 64, for pointers on choosing colors for hooking projects.

2. Place the tulle over the pattern.

Red for Framing

Pin the tulle to the pattern, placing pins alongside the pattern lines to be traced.

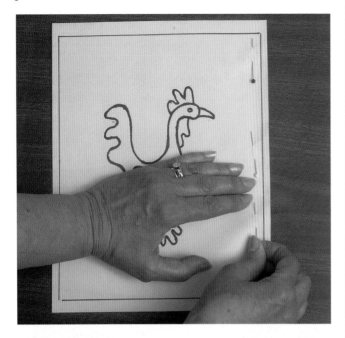

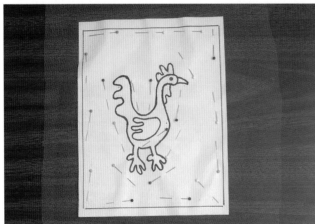

3. Using the permanent marker, lightly trace the rooster pattern and outside outline onto the tulle. If the tulle stretches out of shape too much, use more pins or a lighter touch.

4. Take out the pins to remove the tulle from the pattern.

5. Line up the straight outside edges of the tulle pattern and the pencil outline on the backing and pin in place.

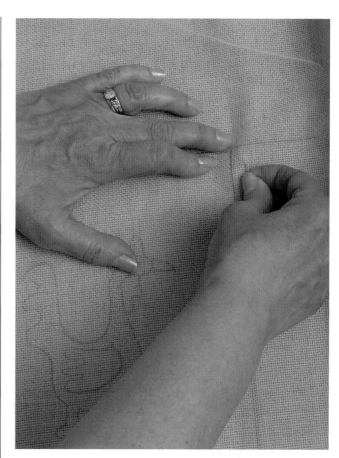

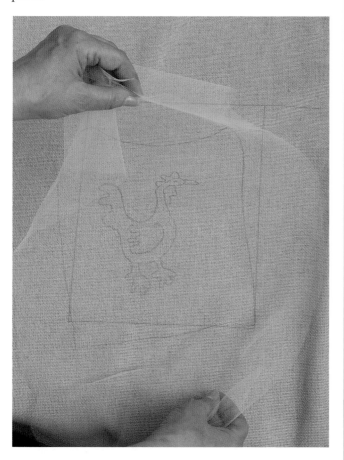

Place pins alongside the pattern lines to be traced.

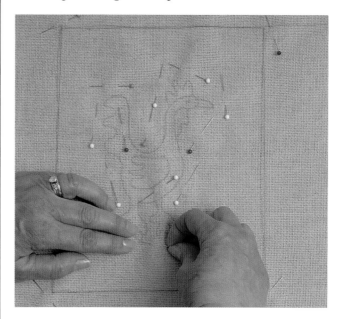

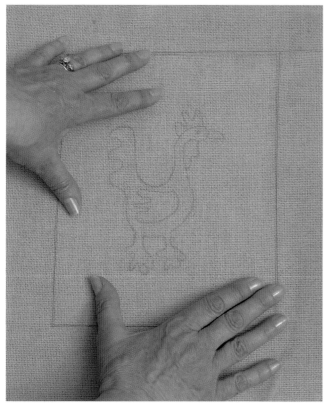

6. With the permanent marker, trace *only* the rooster pattern onto the backing. Do not trace the outside border. It's already there in pencil. Since the background won't be hooked, using a permanent marker along the edge might leave lines that could show along the inside edge of the picture frame.

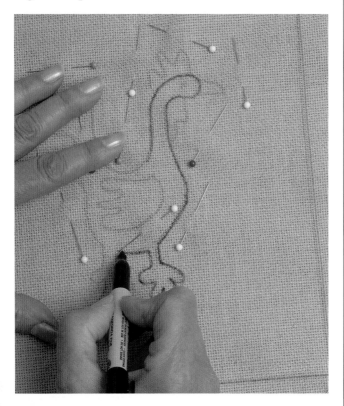

7. Remove the pins to remove the tulle from the backing.

8. To prevent fraying of the edges of the backing fabric while you work, whip the raw edges by hand (one stitch every $1/2$ inch or so) or fold a piece of masking tape over them.

To whip the raw edges, use a needle and any color or type of thread. Cut a length of thread about 30 inches long. Thread the needle and pull 5 to 6 inches through the needle eye. Knot the end of the longer thread. Starting anywhere along the backing edge, insert the needle through the underside of the backing, about $1/2$ inch from the edge. Pull the needle and thread until the knot catches. About $1/2$ inch to the right of where you first inserted the needle, insert the needle again from the back. Draw the thread through until the thread between the two places you inserted the needle rests on the edge of the backing. Continue whipping around the backing until you reach the place where you started, rethreading the needle with more thread as needed.

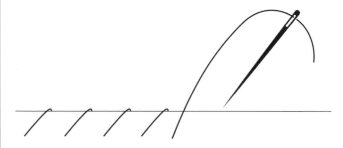

9. Stretch the backing from top to bottom and, holding it taut, place it on the hooking frame, centering the pattern and lining up the straight edges of the pattern with the edges of the frame.

10. Grip the sides of the backing, and lifting slightly, stretch them taut and resettle the backing on the frame. You may need to lift and tug the corners as well to make sure the backing is square in the frame and the pattern is squarely centered in it.

11. When you've selected your wool for hooking, determine the lengthwise grain. If the fabric still has the woven edge, or "selvage," along one or both sides, it follows the straight grain of fabric. (Selvage is usually a little coarser than the rest of the fabric and has no threads that could ravel. The selvage itself can be cut into strips and hooked for special textural effects.)

12. If there is no selvage on the fabric, you can determine the straight grain by stretching it in your hands. If there are a lot of ripples, you're stretching it on the bias, not on the straight grain. Tear your fabric to find the straight grain and cut from there. With wool that has woven-in designs such as checks and plaids, the pattern will follow the straight grain.

13. If the threads of the stretched wool fabric all seem to be running straight between your stretched hands, but you still have quite a few ripples, you are probably stretching it on the crosswise grain. Wool strips cut along this direction are acceptable for wider cuts such as #8, but will not hold together as well when used for narrower cuts such as #3 and #4.

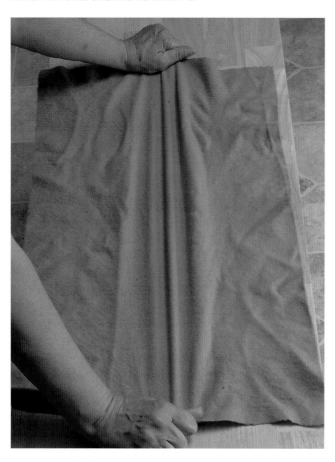

14. When you stretch fabric on the lengthwise grain, you will have the fewest ripples.

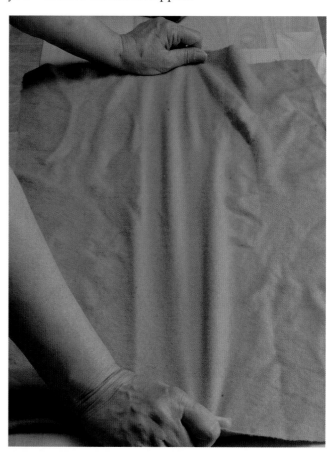

15. You won't need many strips to hook *Red*, and most of them are #8 cut ($^1/_4$ inch) so you can tear the wool in $^1/_2$-inch strips and then use scissors to cut each $^1/_2$-inch strip into two $^1/_4$-inch strips. This will work well if you have good quality wool that is firmly woven instead of loosely woven. If you don't want to tear the wool, cut all the $^1/_4$-inch strips with scissors, following the grain of the fabric, or use a cutting machine. (See chapter 4, page 65, for instructions on how to use a cutting machine.)

Below, a 2-inch strip of fabric is torn and then run through a cutting machine to make strips.

You can make the strips as long as the length of fabric you're using. Hooking is unlike hand-sewing and embroidery in that the strips don't have to be drawn through fabric many times, wearing them out. A strip is pulled through the backing only once to form a loop.

16. For the #4 (¹/₈ inch) strips for the beak, comb, and wattle, use a small pair of scissors to cut ¹/₄-inch strips in half lengthwise, or use a cutting machine with a #4 cutter head.

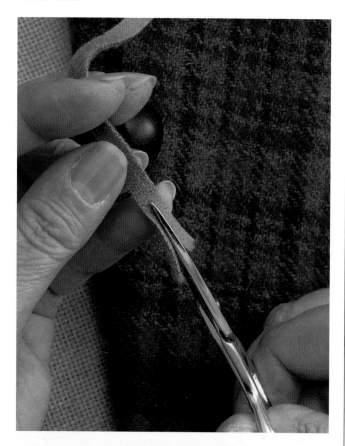

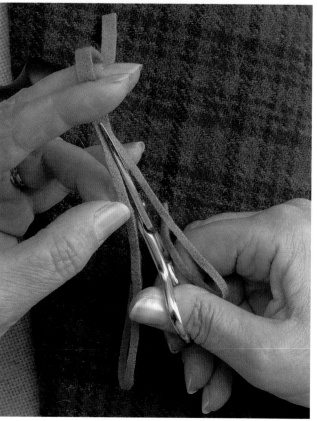

Cut as You Go

Instead of preparing all the strips ahead of time, it's better to cut as you go. This allows you to break up the cutting task, and you won't wind up cutting too much and wasting fabric.

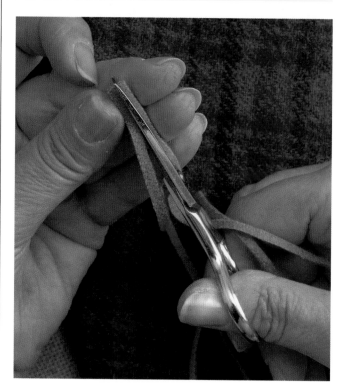

17. Hooking almost always begins in the center of the rug because hooking tends to stretch the backing a bit. Hooking from the center outward stretches the backing more evenly. Outline the wing with #8 cut (¹/₄ inch) strips of gold check wool, keeping inside the line of the wing pattern. Unless you want to change a design, always hook within the lines to maintain the shape and size of designs.

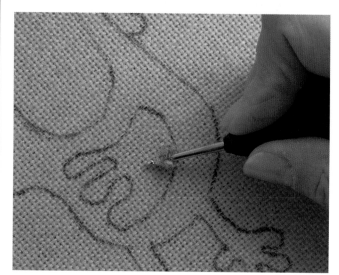

Then fill in the center of the wing with more loops. You can go back and forth, up and down, or around following the outlines, until you've completely filled in the shape.

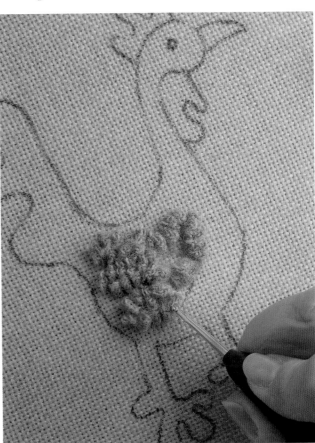

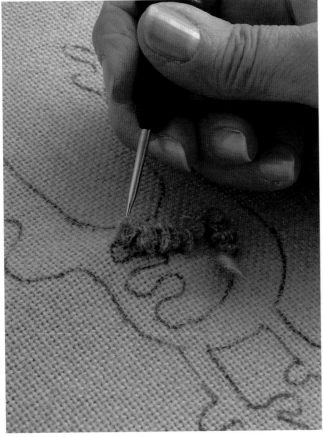

18. Outline the body, head, and neck in #8 cut red plaid.

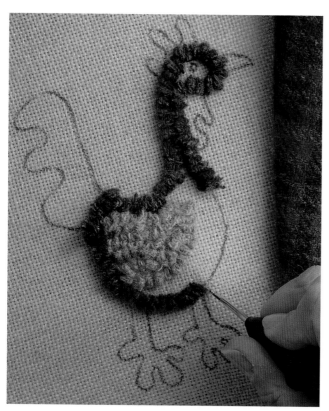

Fill in, following the outside contours of the body, but leaving the eye area unhooked.

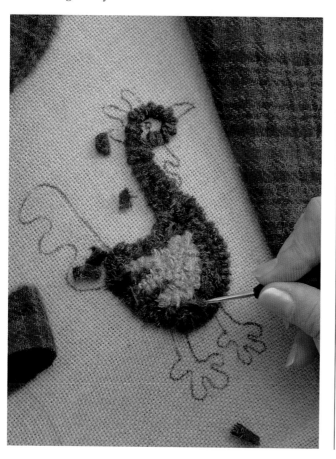

19. To hook the eye, pull the end of a #8-cut gold strip up through the backing.

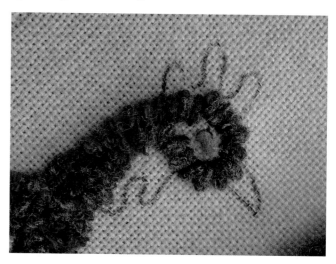

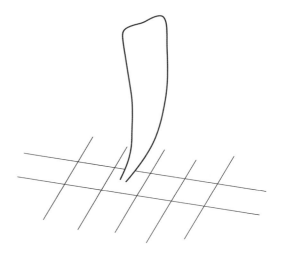

20. Right next to it, hook one gold loop.

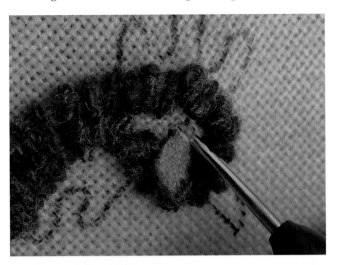

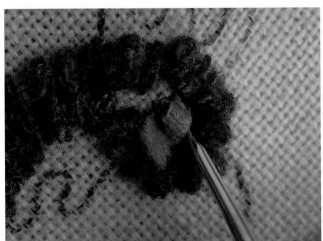

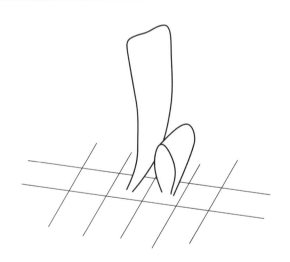

21. Behind the first strip you pulled up, on the other side from the loop, pull up another gold loop in the same hole you used to pull up the first strip.

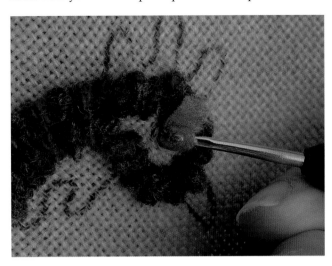

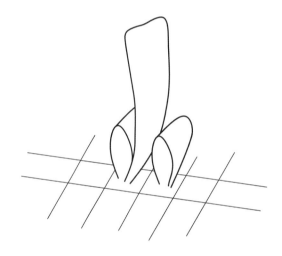

22. Cut the last loop in two at its top. Pull out the remainder of the strip from the underside of the backing.

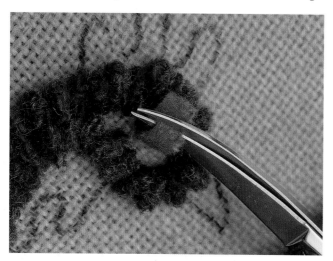

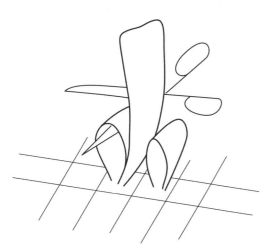

23. Cut off the top of the strip you pulled up first, level with the top of the remaining loop.

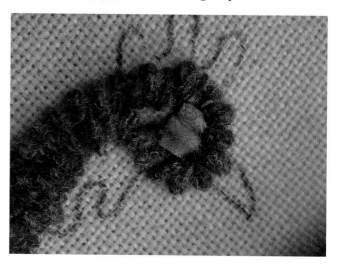

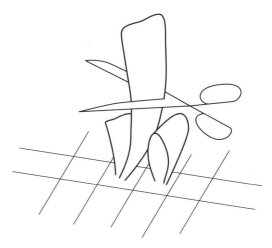

You will now have one loop and two cut ends for the eye.

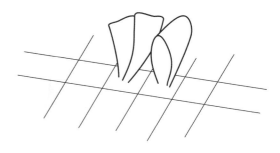

24. Finish hooking the body color around the eye.

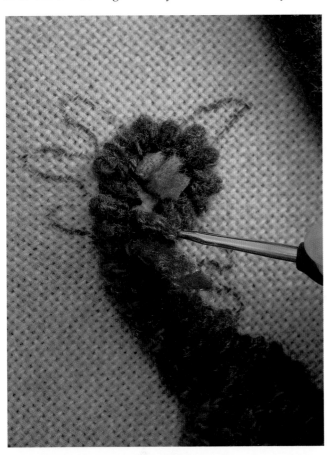

Hook close to the eye to nudge the loop and cut strip ends of the eye closer together to make it smaller and rounder.

Working with Two or More Strip Widths

As a general rule, strips should be hooked as high as they are wide; that is, the loop height of #8 cut (¹/₄ inch) strips should be ¹/₄ inch. However, when using two or more different strip widths, such as #8 and #4 (¹/₈ inch) in this project, always hook the narrower strip as high as the wider strip.

25. Hook the beak in gold #4 cut (¹/₈ inch).

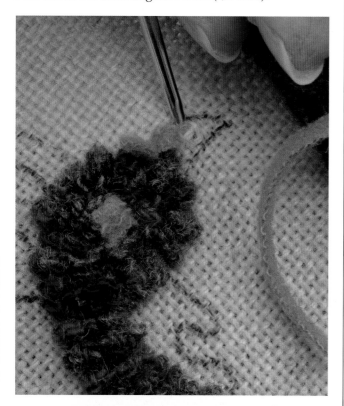

To form the point of the beak, twist the loop one quarter turn so that its cut edge forms the point.

26. To hook the tail, use #8 cuts to outline and fill each section.

Use solid gold for the middle section.

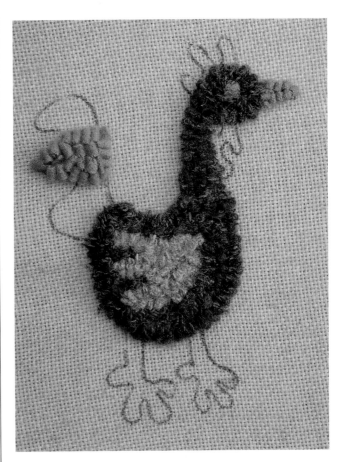

Hook the upper and lower sections of the tail in rust, first outlining and then filling in each section.

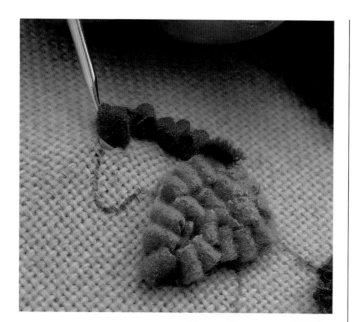

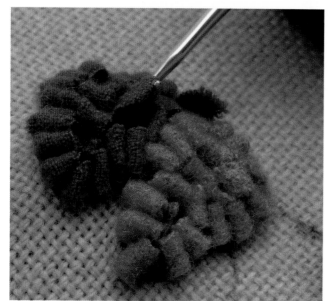

27. With #4 cut strips of rust, outline the comb and wattle and fill in.

28. Hook the feet in #8 cut solid gold by hooking down from the body and angling out.

29. Steaming will level out the bumpiness of the completed hooking. For this small piece, you can use a single bath towel. Completely wet the towel and wring it out. It should be wet but not dripping. Lay the towel on the ironing board with half of it hanging off the side of the ironing board, and place the hooked piece facedown on the towel.

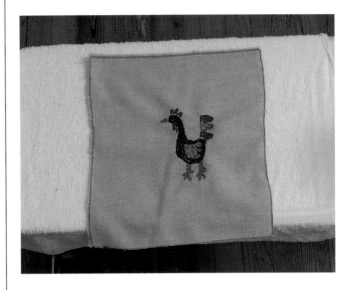

30. Fold the remaining half of the towel over the hooked piece.

31. Preheat the iron to the "high" setting. Without moving the iron from side to side, place it on top of the towel-hooking-towel sandwich. Leave the iron in place until steam has nearly stopped rising. (Overheating and melting the polyester backing is extremely unlikely since it's protected by the wet towels, but don't leave the iron in one spot too long. You can always resteam, but you can't unmelt.)

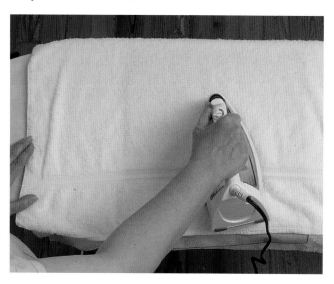

32. Lift the iron and move it to another section. Continue this until the entire hooked piece has been steamed. Never go back and forth with the iron as when ironing a shirt.

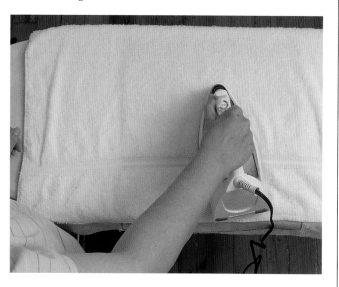

33. Allow the hooked piece to dry flat, face up. If some lumpiness still remains, try steaming again. If that doesn't help, your hooking may be too tight. It may be necessary to remove some of it and rehook it more loosely. See chapter 2, step 14, for instructions on how to remove loops.

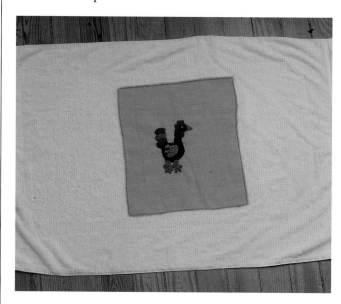

4

Bowl of Flowers Table Mat

Rug hookers often use colors outside the realm of nature to suit the design of a rug. Sometimes a particularly luscious piece of wool will inspire their hues. Shading comes into play in the colors of the flowers and the subtle variations in the background.

The mat is hooked entirely in #8 cut ($^1/_4$ inch), a wide cut that puts this mat into the category of "primitive." *Bowl of Flowers* is intended as a table mat, though its $22^1/_2$ x 10-inch dimensions can be enlarged to rug size if you prefer. Because a table mat isn't subject to the wear of a rug underfoot, the edges are turned under and finished with binding tape. Finishing the edges for a rug is covered in chapter 5, pages 100–105.

BOWL OF FLOWERS

Enlarge pattern to
22 ½ x 10 inches

Pencil

Tape measure or yardstick

Monk's cloth for backing:
  26^1/$_2$ x 14 inches

Bridal tulle: 25 x 12 inches

Quilter or dressmaker pins

Permanent marker, black

Sewing machine with zigzag
  (optional) and thread

Masking tape (optional)

Cotton binding tape: 2 yards

Wool fabric (swatches on page 64)*

  Purple tweed (right and left flower centers):
    1 x 29 inches

  Medium purple-blue (right and left flower
    petals): 2 x 29 inches

  Light purple (right and left flower petals):
    2 x 29 inches

  Beige plaid (stems): 2 x 29 inches

  Teal (outside tulip petals): 1 x 29 inches

  Brown and teal tweed (center tulip petals):
    1 x 29 inches

  Green heather (leaves for center flower):
    1 x 29 inches

  Large green plaid (all other leaves):
    2 x 29 inches

  Red and gold pattern (center flower strips):
    1 x 29 inches

  Gold heather (center flower petals):
    2 x 29 inches

  Red and black honeycomb (center flower
    center): 1 x 29 inches

  Gold-green-brown stripe (bowl):
    4 x 29 inches

  Brown-burgundy plaid (background):
    35 x 29 inches

Dressmaker shears

Cutting machine with #8 wheel (optional)

Hook: medium or coarse

Hooking frame

Small scissors

Buttonhole twist thread or quilting thread and
  needle

Ironing board and iron

Old towels (2)

* The wool fabric doesn't need to be 29 inches long. For example, 4 x 29 inches could be 8 x 14^1/$_2$ inches or another
  dimension, as long as you have about 116 square inches (4 x 29 = 116; 8 x 14^1/$_2$ = 116).

1. Have the pattern enlarged to 22¹/₂ x 10 inches at a copy shop.

2. Leaving a 2-inch border all around, use a pencil and tape measure or yardstick (for measuring) to draw the 22¹/₂ x 10-inch outline of the pattern onto the backing fabric. Be careful to draw along the grain (the direction of the threads) of the fabric. Backings for rug hooking have prominent grain, and you should be able to easily trail the pencil tip along the grain of fabric (in the "trench" between threads) without having to use a straight edge for help. The yardstick is only for measuring. To aid in sewing on the binding, extend the outside lines of the border an inch or so (not shown).

3. Pin the tulle to the pattern.

4. Using the permanent marker, lightly trace the pattern and outside outline onto the tulle. If the tulle stretches out of shape too much, add more pins and use a lighter touch.

5. Take out the pins to remove the tulle from the pattern.

Bowl of Flowers Table Mat

6. Line up the straight outside edges of the tulle pattern and the pencil outline on the backing.

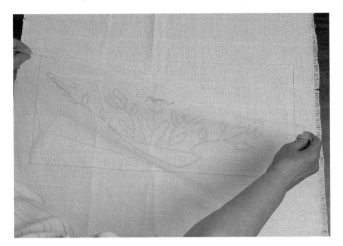

7. Pin the tulle in place.

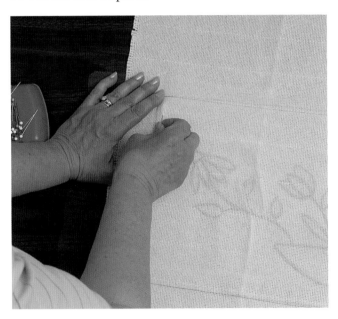

8. With the permanent marker, trace the pattern onto the backing, including the outside lines. Extend the outside lines beyond the corners about $1/2$ inch to aid in sewing on the binding tape.

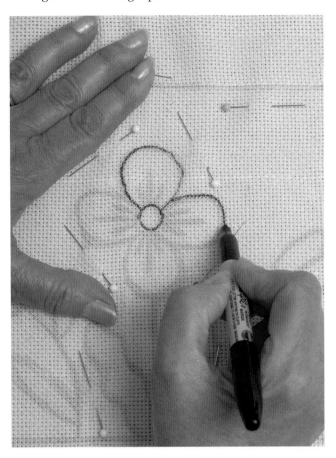

9. Remove the pins to remove the tulle from the backing.

10. To prevent fraying of the edges of the backing fabric while you work, zigzag the raw edges of the backing with a sewing machine. You may want to zigzag before you cut off any excess backing.

11. On the front of the backing, starting near the middle of an edge of the pattern border line, lay the binding tape along the inside edge of the border line.

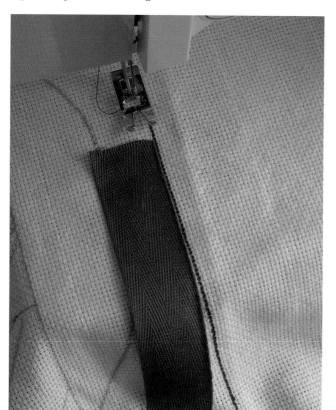

12. Turn up about $1/2$ inch of the end of the binding tape.

13. Using a straight stitch on the sewing machine (or by hand), begin sewing the binding tape to the backing along the inside edge of the border line, keeping the stitching near the edge of the binding tape and the binding tape straight along the border.

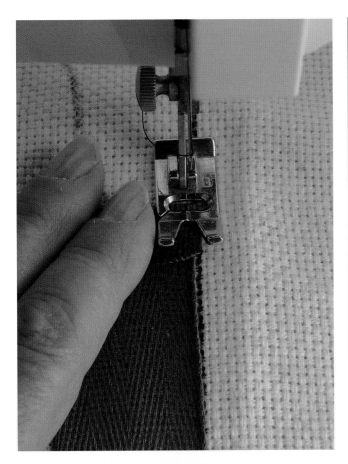

14. When you near a corner, watch for the line you extended past the edge of the pattern.

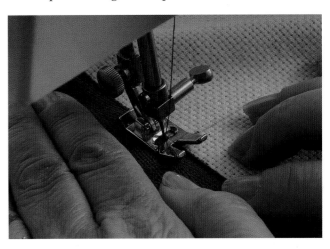

15. When the needle is even with the extended line to the right, keep the needle down and raise the presser foot.

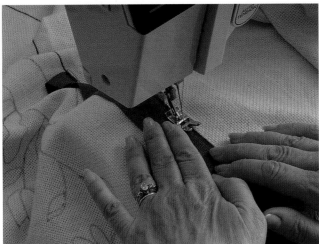

16. Pivoting on the needle, turn the backing counterclockwise so that the next edge is ready to be sewn.

17. Bring the binding tape around so that it again lines up with the inside edge of the border. (The binding tape will rise up to the left.)

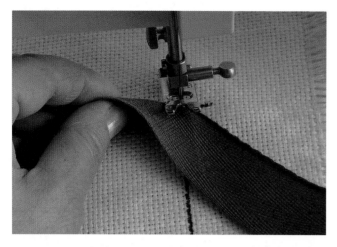

18. Lower the presser foot and continue stitching the binding tape.

Repeat steps 14 through 18 at each corner.

19. Stop about 1 inch from where you started.

Cut the tape about 1½ inches longer than you need to reach the starting point.

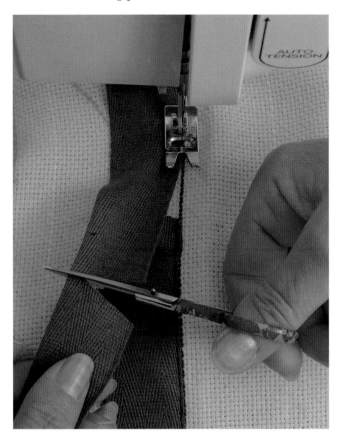

20. Fold the cut end up about ½ inch.

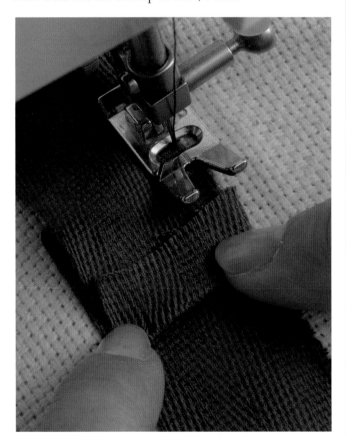

21. Continue stitching, holding the folds in place as you stitch over them.

61

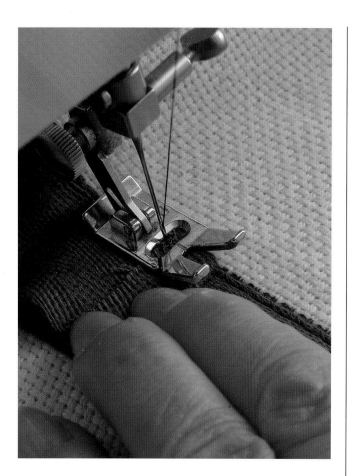

23. Turn the mat facedown and zigzag about 1 1/2 inches outside the binding tape, narrowing to about 1 inch on the corners.

22. Backstitch to secure the thread, and cut the thread.

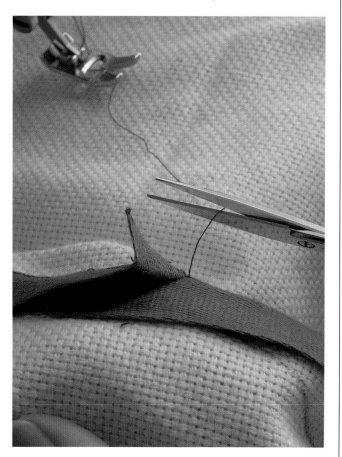

Narrowing to 1 inch and zigzagging diagonally across the corner will decrease the amount of backing fabric that must be folded in when the edge is finished.

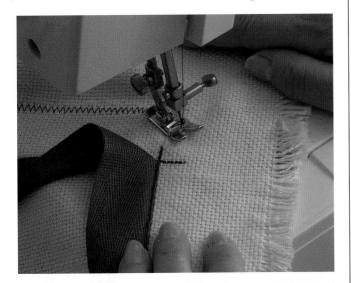

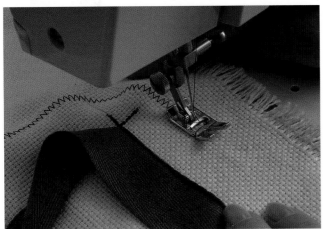

24. Stretch the backing from top to bottom and, holding it taut, place it on the hooking frame, centering the pattern and lining up the straight edges of the pattern with the edges of the frame. If your hooking frame is smaller than the pattern, you will need to shift the mat on the frame to work on different areas.

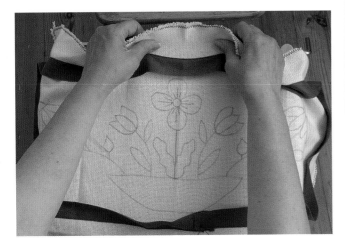

25. Stretch and pull the sides and corners until the backing is taut and the pattern is straight.

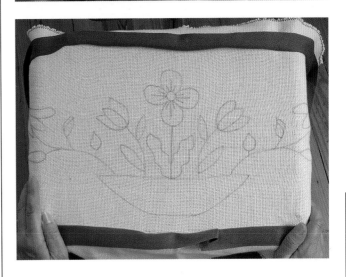

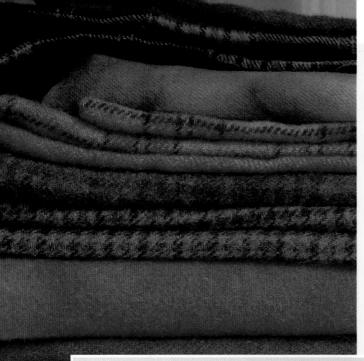

Selecting Wool Colors

The fabric choices are muted for this project. If you'd like to try different colors, gather samples together to make sure they work well with each other. If there's one color that stands out too much, replace it with another. In the photo at right, the light blue stands out too much. The combination of colors would be better without it. Keep experimenting until the combination pleases you, and all the colors harmonize with each other. Hooked rugs (and mats) last a long time and will probably outlast several decorating schemes. When you choose colors, select them for the rug, not for the room.

26. When you've selected your wool for hooking, determine the lengthwise grain. (See chapter 3, steps 11 to 14.)

27. All the strips are #8 cut ($^1/_4$ inch). Either tear and cut with scissors as in chapter 2, steps 3 through 6, or use a cutting machine, as described on the next page.

28. For the center flower, begin by hooking the red and black honeycomb center.

29. Hook the lines radiating from the center in the red and gold pattern.

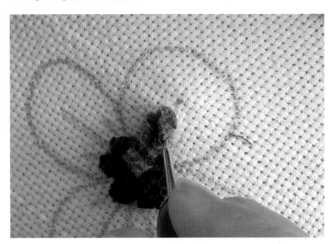

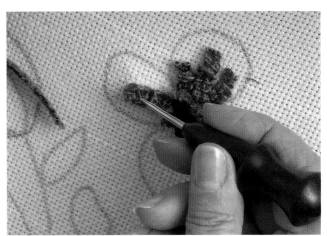

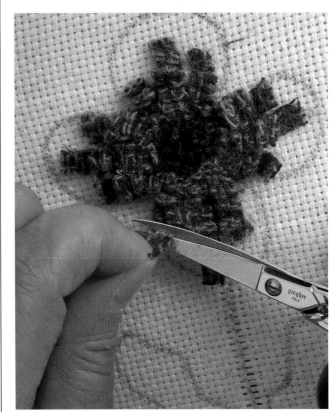

How to Use a Cutting Machine

Individual machines vary as to how to change cutter heads, so you'll need to rely on the instructions that come with the machine for that information. The cutting process itself, however, is similar for all machines.

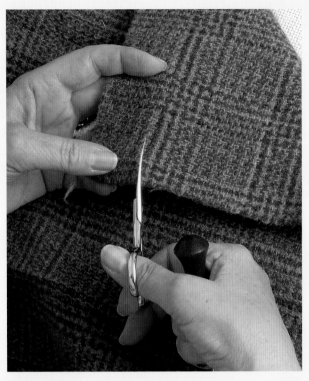

First, make a small cut along the straight grain of fabric. For just a few strips, make the snip 1 inch from the edge of the fabric. For more strips, snip it up to 4 inches from the edge.

Hold the long straight edge of the fabric alongside the guide on the right side of the feeding plate of the machine and with the short end of the fabric against the cutting mechanism. Turn the crank with your right hand until the cutter heads begin cutting the fabric. With your left hand, gently guide the fabric so that the right edge of it remains in contact with the machine's guide to the right of the fabric.

Starting at the snipped place, tear the fabric apart. The tear will occur along the straight grain, assuring that the strips you cut with the machine will also be on the straight grain.

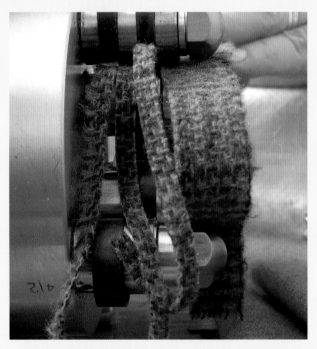

As the strips begin to exit the back of the machine, you may need to reach around with your left hand to catch the strips and keep them from winding around the cutter head or falling to the floor.

Organizing Wool Strips

To keep strips from tangling and getting mixed in with different colors, gather each color together and tie loosely with another strip.

30. Hook the remainder of the center flower petals in gold heather by outlining and filling. Be sure to fill in between the lines radiating from the center. Notice how the lines recede as you hook around them until they're just subtle hints of color.

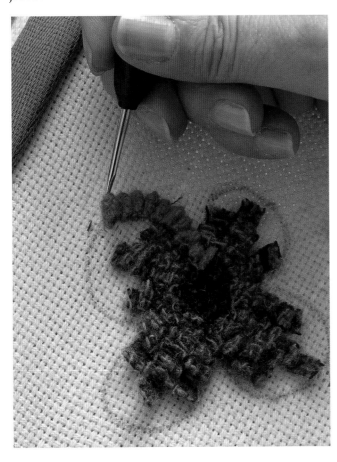

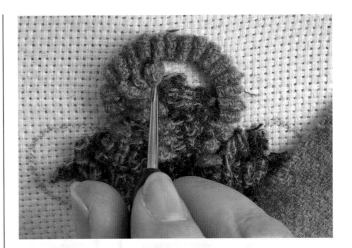

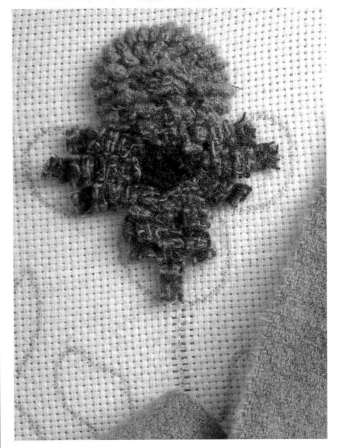

31. Hook the center stem in beige plaid. It's just a single row of loops, hooked on the line—this is one of the exceptions to the general rule to always hook within the lines.

32. Outline and fill the two leaves on either side of the center stem in green heather.

33. For the tulips at left and right, hook the stems in a single row of beige plaid directly on top of the line in the design. Outline and fill the center tulip petals in brown and teal tweed, turning the loop at the top point of each petal to make a point so that the cut edge of the loop is at the point instead of the folded edge.

Don't start or end a strip at the point.

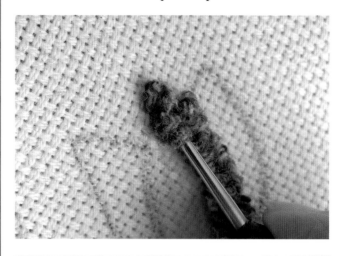

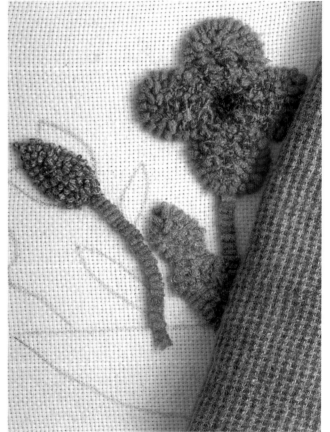

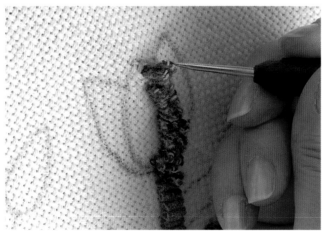

34. Outline and fill the outside tulip petals in teal, again forming a point at the top of each.

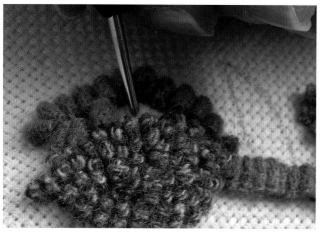

35. Hook the daisy stems.

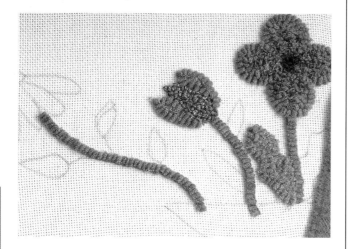

36. For the centers of the daisies at far left and right, begin hooking the purple tweed at the center of the flat bottom, outlining and filling.

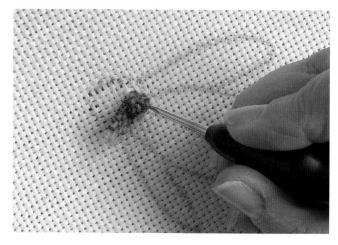

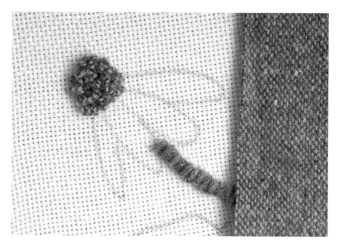

37. Outline and fill the alternating medium blue–purple and light purple daisy petals, remembering to turn a loop to form the point of each.

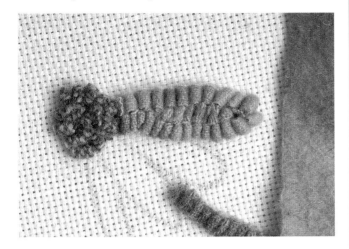

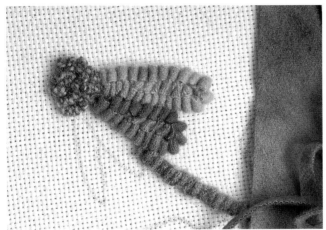

Hiding Cut Ends

Avoid starting a strip on a corner where the cut end will be easier to spot and may fray a bit in an obvious place. Hide the cut end by starting in the middle of a pattern line.

38. Hook the buds with light purple at the tops and outer edges and medium blue–purple at the bottoms and inner edges.

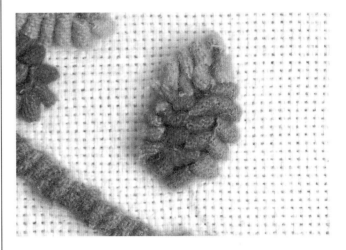

39. Hook the remaining stems in beige plaid and the rest of the leaves in the large green plaid.

40. The bowl is hooked in the gold-green-brown stripe. Outline it first and then fill in, with the fill hooking following along the outline hooking.

41. After the flowers, buds, stems, leaves, and bowl are completed, start filling in the background with the brown-burgundy plaid, first outlining all of the parts you've already hooked. Also outline the outer edge of the piece with the brown-burgundy plaid, hooking very close to the binding tape.

42. To fill in the rest of the background, continue adding rows of outlining around the flowers, buds, stems, leaves, and bowl until the entire backing is filled.

Mix It Up

Many rug hookers find that filling in the background isn't as much fun as hooking the rest of the design. If you feel the same way, alternate outlining the design elements with hooking the background.

Sign Your Work

Always sign and date your hooking. Some rug hookers hide their initials and the year they complete a piece with subtle colors worked into a border or the background. Others choose less subtle colors so their initials and the year stand out. Some stitch a piece of cloth to the back with name or initials and date in embroidery or permanent ink.

43. Beginning along one side, fold the edge of the backing under.

44. Lay the binding tape over the top of the folded backing.

45. With needle and thread, whip stitch the binding tape to the backing, being careful to catch the backing with the needle, not just the bottoms of the wool loops. Stitches should be about $^1/_2$ inch apart.

46. Stop whipping about 3 inches from the corner.

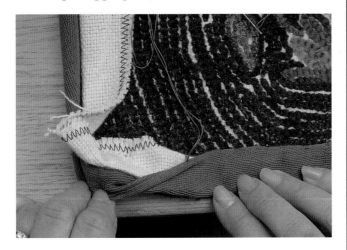

47. To miter the corner of the backing, first turn the backing up diagonally at the corner.

48. Fold it diagonally toward the rug.

49. Pin in place.

50. Refold the side edge of the backing, place it over the corner fold, and pin it in place.

51. Fold over the edge of the backing along the other side.

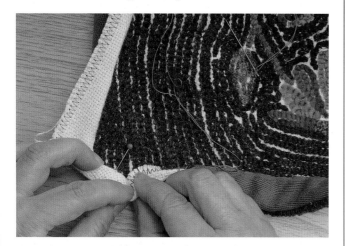

52. Fold it toward the rug and pin it in place.

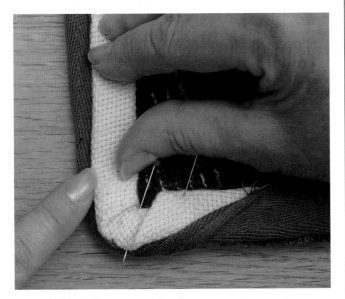

53. Place the binding over the corner and pull the slack to the side you haven't stitched yet.

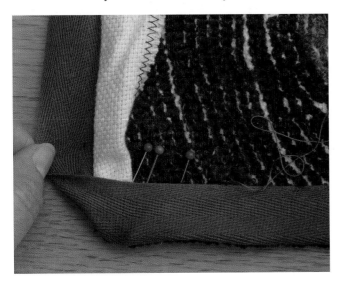

54. Fold the slack toward the rug, forming a diagonal fold in the corner. Pin in place.

55. Resume whip stitching to the corner. At the corner, stitch the two overlapping edges of the binding tape together. Remove the pin.

56. Continue whip stitching along each side, with the backing folded under, and repeat mitering at each corner.

57. Pin and stitch together the fold where the two ends of the binding tape meet.

59. Put the needle through the backing where the thread end will be concealed by the binding tape. Clip the thread where it comes out of the backing. Whip the remainder of the binding tape to the rug backing.

58. Secure the thread by pulling it partially through the edge of the binding tape, leaving a small loop of thread behind. Put the needle through the loop, then pull the thread so the loop tightens around the loose end of the thread. Repeat.

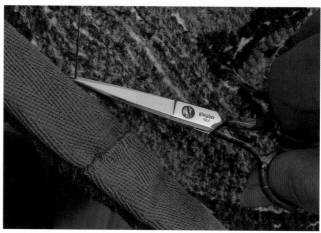

60. Steam the mat to make it lie flat. Place a wet, wrung-out towel on the ironing board, and lay the mat, facedown, on the towel.

61. Cover it with another wet, wrung-out towel.

62. Preheat the iron to the "wool" or "high" setting. Place the iron on top of the towel-hooking-towel sandwich. Leave the iron in place until steam has nearly stopped rising. Do not move the iron over the surface.

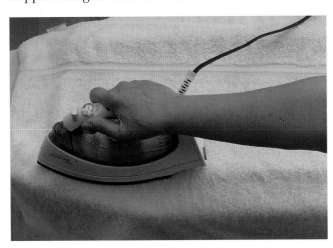

63. Lift the iron and move it to another section. Continue this until the entire hooked piece has been steamed.

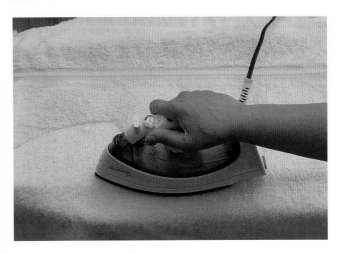

64. Allow the mat to dry flat, face up. If some lumpiness still remains, try steaming again. If that doesn't help, the hooking may be too tight. It may be necessary to remove some of it and rehook it more loosely. See chapter 2, step 14, to see how to remove loops.

79

5

Back Home Again Rug

Sail away with *Back Home Again*. The striking blue and white colors and the charming island details make this rug a standout design. You'll learn how to make crisp square corners for the border. Dimensions are $20^{1}/_{2}$ x 16 inches.

BACK HOME AGAIN

Enlarge pattern to 20½ x 16 inches

TOOLS AND MATERIALS

Pencil

Tape measure or yardstick

Linen backing: 30$^1/_2$ x 26 inches

Bridal tulle: 22$^1/_2$ x 18 inches

Quilter or dressmaker pins

Permanent marker, black

Sewing machine with zigzag (optional) and thread

Masking tape (optional)

Wool fabric (swatches on page 85)*

   White (center sails, small boat sail, lighthouse): 11 x 29 inches

   Off-white (outer sails): 7 x 29 inches

   Gold-brown (masts): 3 x 29 inches

   Red (flag, lighthouse door, buoy): 2 x 29 inches

   Black (boat, rigging, house windows, lighthouse window, roof, small boat tether line): 10 x 29 inches

Gray (waves): 6 x 29 inches

Light orange (house side): 1 x 29 inches

Medium orange (house front): 1 x 29 inches

Camel (house roof, edge): 1 x 29 inches

Medium gold (tree leaves): 1 x 29 inches

Dark brown (tree trunk on left, tree bottom on right, small boat mast): 1 x 29 inches

Dark green–black check (tree leaves on right): 2 x 29 inches

Medium green (grass), 2 different plaids: 5 x 29 inches each

Bright gold (small boat, light in lighthouse): 1 x 29 inches

Blue-gray honeycomb (background water): 36 x 29 inches

Dressmaker shears

Cutting machine with #8 and #4 wheels (optional)

Hook: medium

Hooking frame

Small scissors

Ironing board and iron

Old towels (2)

Cotton piping, $^1/_4$ inch: 2$^1/_4$ yards

Wool yarn to match blue water (not too fuzzy, merino works well): 32 yards

Large-eye needle

Needle-nose pliers

* The wool fabric doesn't need to be 29 inches long. For example, 6 x 29 inches could be 12 x 14$^1/_2$ inches or another dimension, as long as you have about 174 square inches (6 x 29 = 174; 12 x 14$^1/_2$ = 174). Sizes are approximate.

Instructions

1. Have the pattern enlarged to 20$\frac{1}{2}$ x 16 inches at a copy shop.

2. Leaving a 5-inch border all around, use a pencil and tape measure or yardstick (for measuring) to draw the 20$\frac{1}{2}$ x 16-inch outline of the pattern onto the backing fabric. Be careful to draw along the grain (the direction of the threads) of the fabric.

3. Pin the tulle to the pattern.

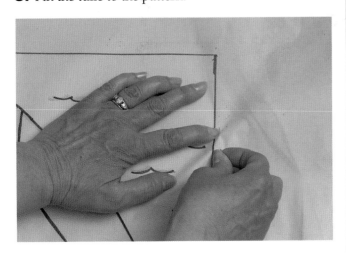

4. Using the permanent marker, lightly trace the pattern and outside outline onto the tulle. If the tulle stretches out of shape too much, add more pins and use a lighter touch.

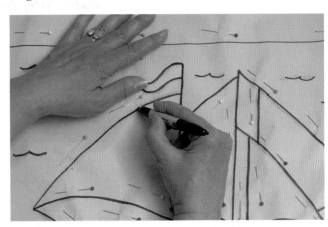

5. Take out the pins to remove the tulle from the pattern.
  Line up the straight outside edges of the tulle pattern and the pencil outline on the backing and pin in place.

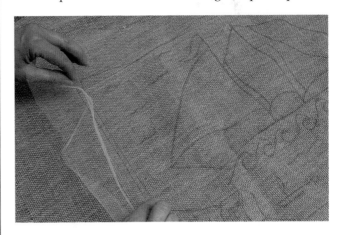

6. With the permanent marker, trace the pattern onto the backing.

7. Remove the pins to remove the tulle from the backing.

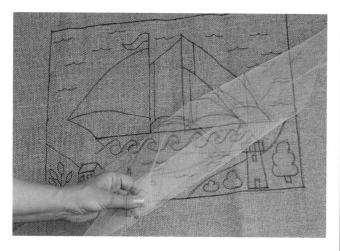

8. Zigzag the raw edges of the backing and stretch the backing on a frame.

9. To cut the #4-cut ($^1/_8$ inch) strips for the lighthouse and rigging, cut #8-cut strips in half lengthwise, or use a cutting machine with a #4 cutting head.

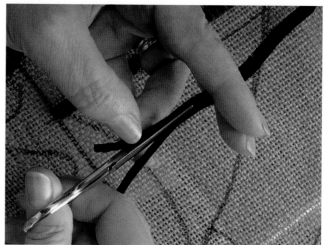

Wool Colors

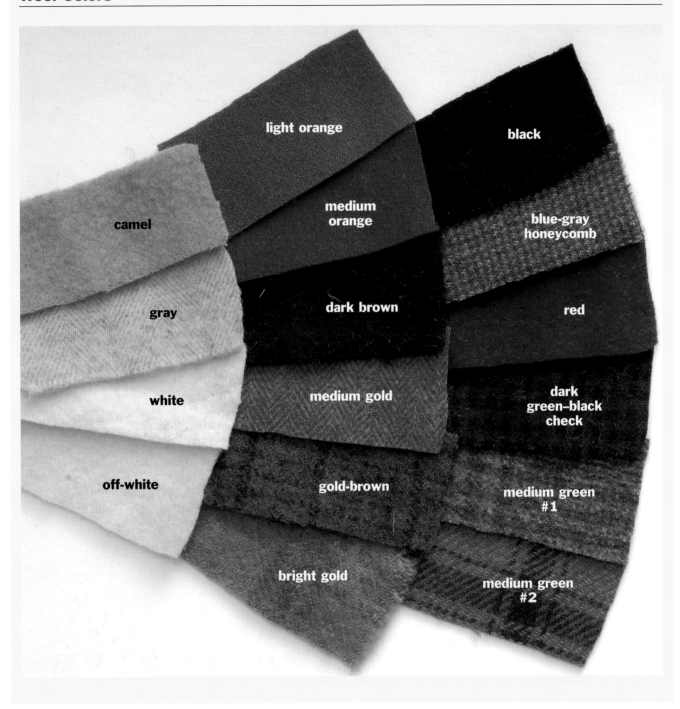

camel

light orange

black

medium orange

gray

blue-gray honeycomb

dark brown

red

white

medium gold

dark green–black check

off-white

gold-brown

medium green #1

bright gold

medium green #2

10. First hook the gold-brown masts, using a single row of loops on the pattern lines.

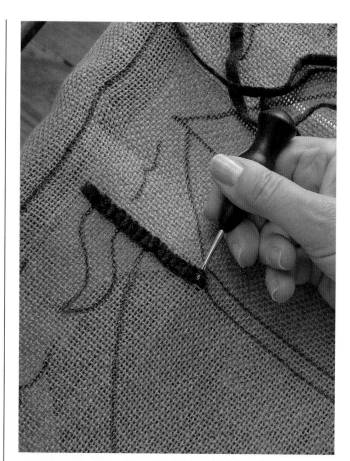

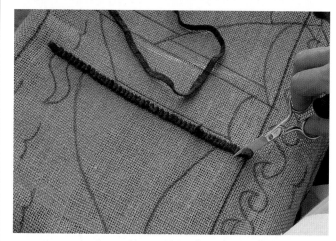

11. Using black #4 cut (refer to step 9) in $^1/_4$ inch-high loops, hook the line of rigging to the middle right of the right mast in a single row, hooking directly on the line.

12. Hook the white sail between the masts by outlining and filling with vertical rows.

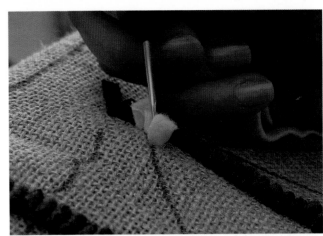

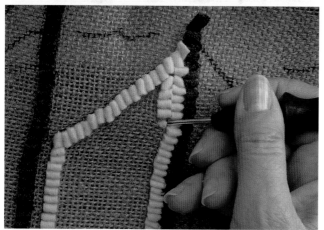

13. Hook the white sail to the lower right of the right mast by outlining and filling with vertical rows, as in step 12.

14. Hook the two outer off-white sails by outlining and then filling with diagonal rows that follow the outer edges of the sails.

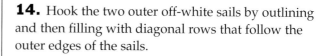

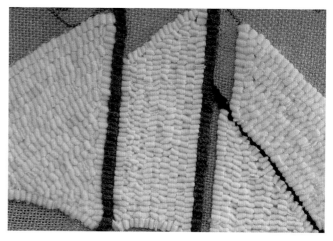

Avoiding Hand Fatigue

As you see the pattern evolve into lush wooly textures and colors, the temptation is often great to keep hooking until your hands start complaining. These exercises will refresh them so you can keep going.

Squeeze a squeeze ball several times.

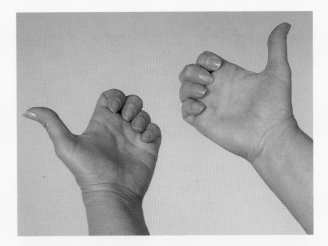

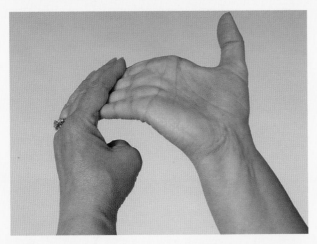

Gently press your fingers back to stretch them and your wrist.

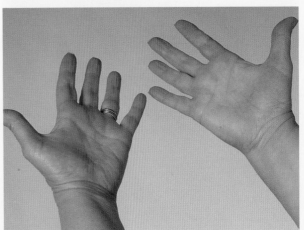

Fold your fingers down tightly, then spread them wide.

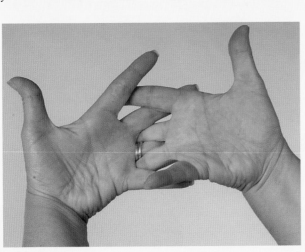

Lock fingers together and bend them back.

15. Finish hooking all the rigging in #4 cut black ($^1/_4$-inch-high loops), in the following order: top of right mast to sail, bottom of right sail to ship's hull, bottom of left sail to ship's hull. You may need to shift the backing on the frame to hook the far right and far left rigging.

16. Hook the red flag at the top of the left mast by outlining and filling.

90

17. Hook the gray waves beneath the ship's hull, turning the last loop on the crest of each wave to make a point, then reversing hooking direction to complete each section of wave. Also hook the waves in the background water.

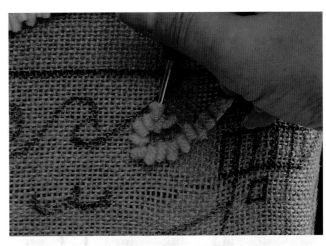

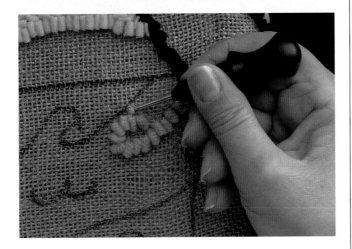

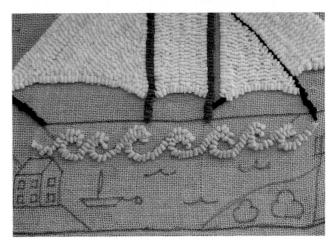

18. In black, outline the ship's hull and the top of the waves beneath it, then fill.

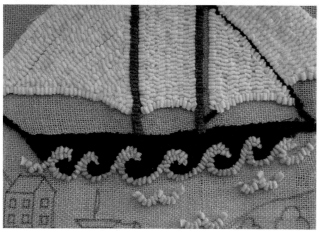

19. Hook the black windows of the house at lower left.

20. Hook the house roof in camel.

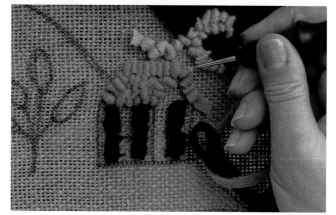

21. Cut a ¼-inch camel strip in two lengthwise to hook the line between the side and front of the house.

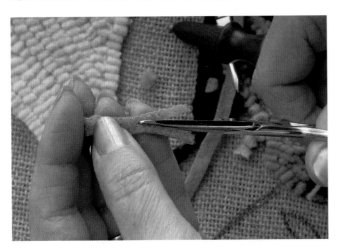

22. Hook directly on top of the line.

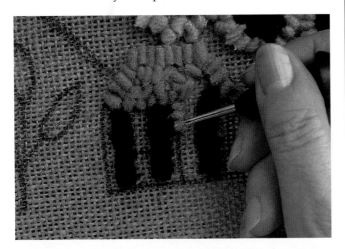

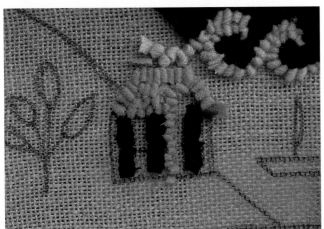

23. With the light orange, hook the side of the house.

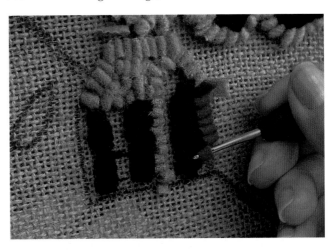

Note that there are two loops between the upper and lower windows.

24. Hook the front in medium orange, again putting two loops between the upper and lower windows.

93

25. Use dark brown to hook the tree trunk.

26. The tree foliage is hooked in medium gold.

27. Hook the bright gold hull, dark brown mast, and white sail of the tiny boat at the bottom center. Hook its tether line in black and the red buoy. Don't be concerned if the small details of this boat seem to balloon out of proportion. Hooking the background water around them will rein them in.

28. Outline the grass at left and fill.

29. Begin the island at right by hooking the black lighthouse window and red door.

30. Hook the lighthouse body with white vertical lines, the area surrounding the lights at top in #4 cut ($^1/_8$ inch) black (in $^1/_4$-inch-high loops), and the lights in bright gold. Complete the roof with black.

31. Hook the dark brown base of the tree at far right.

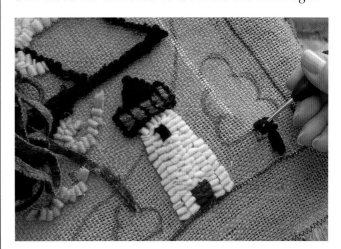

32. The foliage of the trees at right is hooked in dark green. Outline and fill.

33. Outline the lighter green grass and fill.

34. Begin the black border alongside the grass at right. It is one row of hooking.

35. When you come to the corner, follow the directions for hooking square corners (see sidebar on page 98), and continue hooking all around the rug.

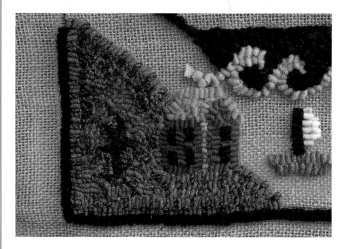

36. Hook the next border line in blue-gray honeycomb in a single row around the rug, following the instructions on the next page for making square corners.

Caring for Hooked Rugs

Hooked rugs can last many generations if they're properly cared for. For routine cleaning, use a vacuum cleaner with an upholstery tool. Don't use a vacuum with a beater bar, as this will quickly wear the rug.

Never submerge the rug in water. If some of the dye colors are unstable, the rug may be ruined. Spot cleaning can be done with a mild solution of Woolite fabric wash and a soft cloth. If the rug is in need of more cleaning, companies that clean oriental rugs are the only professionals who may be able to clean your rug safely. Do not use a dry cleaner.

Don't be afraid to put your rug on the floor. It can withstand normal foot traffic for many years. Avoid places where it would be subject to excessive soiling such as by the front door or kitchen sink.

Never shake the rug; it's too hard on the backing.

To prevent excessive fading, choose a spot where the rug will not be exposed to direct sun.

To store a rug, roll it with the backing side in. Use an old pillowcase or sheet to wrap the rolled-up rug, never plastic.

Hooking Square Corners

To hook a square corner, hook two loops past where the corner turns.

For the next side of the square shape, butt the flat side of the first loop against the cut sides of the extra loops you hooked.

37. Using the blue-gray honeycomb, outline the border, the sails, hulls, and rigging of the large ship, the small ship's sail, hull, tether, and buoy, the gray waves, and the islands.

38. Fill in the blue-gray honeycomb background by hooking straight across the rug horizontally.

39. Trim edges of backing to about 1$^1/_2$ inches, narrowing the edges at the corners to about 1 inch to $^3/_4$ inch. Zigzag the edges.

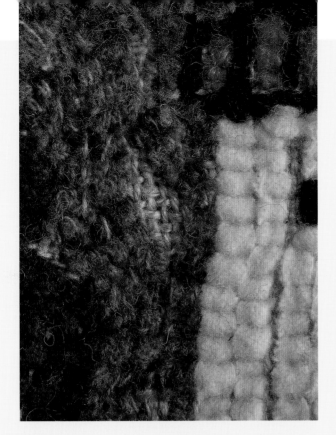

Filling Bare Spaces, or "Holidays"

After the rug is completely hooked, turn it over to check for any places on the backing that are too sparsely hooked, called "holidays." As the rug wears, these will become obvious bare spaces on the front, so they need to be filled in.

Working from the front, fill each holiday with loops. In some cases you may have to remove an area of hooking (see chapter 2, step 20) to rehook it tighter.

From the back, stick a toothpick through each holiday so it will show in the front.

On the back, the bare spot near the lighthouse is now filled.

40. Cut about 8 feet of yarn, and loop the yarn to make it easier to thread the needle.

Pull half of the yarn through the needle so that you're working with a double strand.

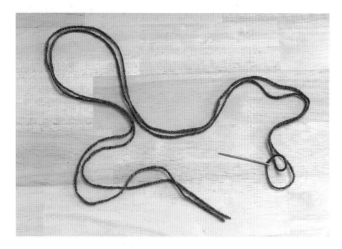

41. Beginning on a straight edge of the front of the rug, at least 4 inches from a corner, roll the backing up over the cord and up to the edge of the hooking.

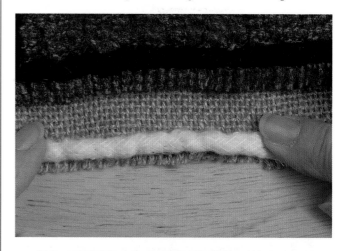

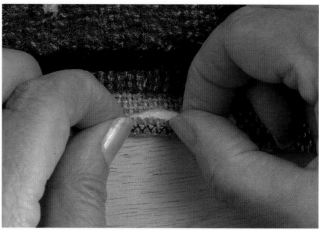

42. From the top, insert the needle in the backing along the edge of the hooking.

43. Pull the yarn through, leaving a tail of yarn about 3 inches long. Place the tail along the edge of the hooking, so it can be rolled up and whipped along with the backing-wrapped cord. If you plan to whip from right to left, place the tail on the left, so that it will be secured when you begin whipping.

44. Begin whipping the yarn snugly around the roll, making sure the yarn completely covers the roll.

45. Make sure the whipping covers right up to the hooking on the bottom of the rug, too. Use the same holes you used for the last row of hooking for whipping.

46. When you're close to running out of yarn, push your needle lengthwise a couple of inches through the whipped edge you've just completed. You may need needle-nose pliers to help you push the needle through the tightly rolled and whipped edge. Bring the needle to the surface and pull the yarn taut. Clip the yarn at the surface of the rolled edge. Rethread the needle and again leave a 3-inch tail in the part of the roll you'll be whipping next.

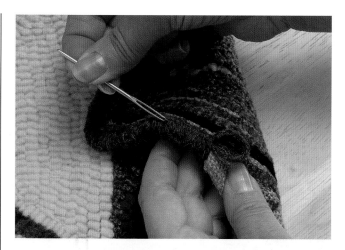

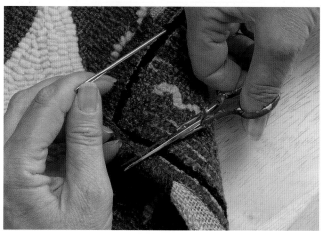

47. As you near a corner, roll the backing up diagonally over the cord.

48. Fold in the "ear" of the backing that formed when you made the diagonal fold.

49. Carefully whip over the "ear" to make sure it is completely covered, and continue to whip toward the corner. To fully cover the roll on the corner, you'll need to make many stitches on the inside edge of the roll, close together, but don't use the same hole in the backing twice. Using each hole once should be enough. To avoid using the same hole twice, make some of your stitches a little further back from the hooking edge and some next to it.

50. When you reach the corner, roll the cord in the backing on the next side. This will form another "ear" where the backing meets the diagonal corner fold. Fold the "ear" in as you did before and whip over it.

51. Continue around the rug, handling each corner as in steps 50 to 53.

103

52. When you near the point where you started, cut the end of the cord so that it will butt up against the beginning of the cord. Then roll the backing over it.

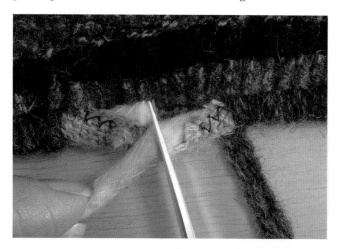

53. Whip to the point where you began.

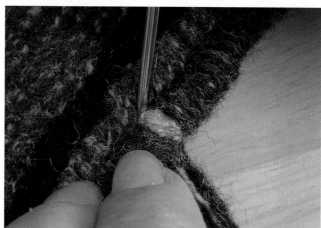

54. Use the pliers to force the needle through the whipped cord you just completed, as in step 46, and cut the yarn off level with the surface.

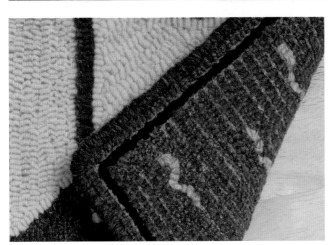

55. Steam the rug to make it lie flat. Place a wet, wrung-out towel on the ironing board, and lay the rug, facedown, on the towel.

56. Cover it with another wet, wrung-out towel.

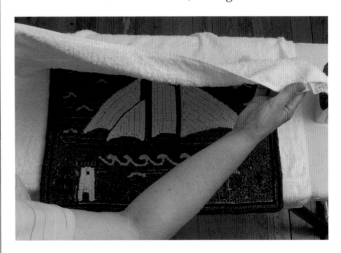

57. Preheat the iron to the "wool" or "high" setting. Without moving the iron from side to side, place it on top of the towel-hooking-towel sandwich. Leave the iron in place until steam has nearly stopped rising.

58. Continue to lift the iron and move it to another section.

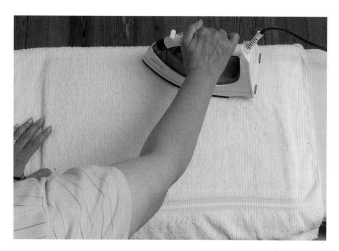

59. Shift the towels and rug so the entire rug can be steamed.

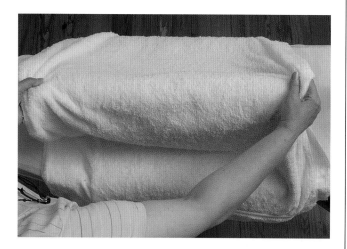

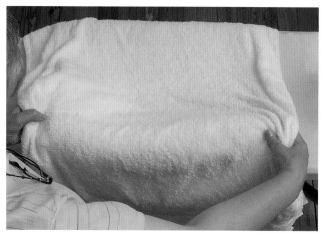

60. Allow the rug to dry flat, face up. If some lumpiness still remains, try steaming again. If that doesn't help, the hooking may be too tight. It may be necessary to remove some of it and rehook it more loosely. (See chapter 2, step 20, to see how to remove loops.)

If you'd prefer to hang your rug to protect those white sails from foot traffic, see chapter 6, pages 118–19.

6

Bird and Bees Rug

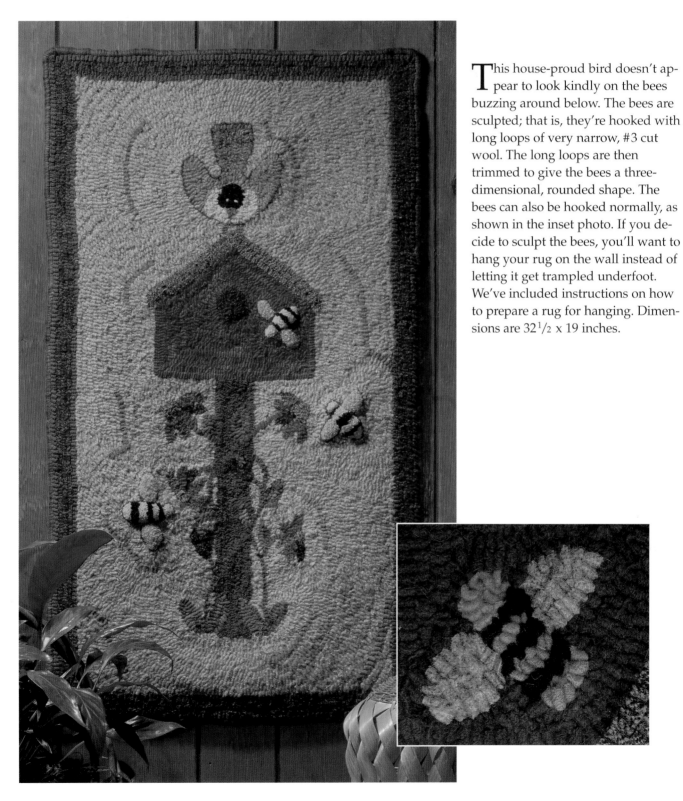

This house-proud bird doesn't appear to look kindly on the bees buzzing around below. The bees are sculpted; that is, they're hooked with long loops of very narrow, #3 cut wool. The long loops are then trimmed to give the bees a three-dimensional, rounded shape. The bees can also be hooked normally, as shown in the inset photo. If you decide to sculpt the bees, you'll want to hang your rug on the wall instead of letting it get trampled underfoot. We've included instructions on how to prepare a rug for hanging. Dimensions are 32$\frac{1}{2}$ x 19 inches.

BIRD AND BEES

Enlarge pattern to 32½ x 19 inches

Pencil

Tape measure or yardstick

Monk's cloth for backing: $42^1/_2$ x 29 inches

Bridal tulle: $34^1/_2$ x 21 inches

Quilter or dressmaker pins

Permanent marker, black

Sewing machine with zigzag (optional) and thread for protecting edges of backing

Masking tape (optional)

Wool fabric (swatches on page 113)*

Maroon (birdhouse hole): 1 x 29 inches

Black (bee stripes, bird head): 1 x 29 inches (4 x 29 inches for the sculpted bees)

Gold (bees): 2 x 29 inches (10 x 29 inches for the sculpted bees)

Gray (bee wings): 1 x 29 inches (20 x 29 inches for the sculpted bees)

Charcoal herringbone (roof, flower centers): 5 x 29 inches

Red (birdhouse): 8 x 29 inches

Red-gold-black check (flowers, buds): 2 x 29 inches

Solid dark gold (flowers): 1 x 29 inches

Red-gold herringbone (flowers): 1 x 29 inches

Solid dark rust (flowers): 1 x 29 inches

Gold-rust heather (flowers): 1 x 29 inches

Light rust (buds, bird legs): 1 x 29 inches

Brown (vines, border): 10 x 29 inches

Green (leaves): 3 x 29 inches

Light gray (bird breast, eyes): 1 x 29 inches

Medium gray (bird wings and back): 2 x 29 inches

Gray plaid (bird tail): 2 x 29 inches

Medium gold herringbone (bird beak): 1 x 29 inches

Blue (pole): 5 x 29 inches

Red plaid (border): 15 x 29 inches

Beige (background): 78 x 29 inches

Medium brown check (background accents): 4 x 29 inches

Dark gray (#4 cut, if needed for outlining bees, bird): 1 x 29 inches

Dressmaker shears

Cutting machine with #8, #4, and #3 wheels (optional)

Hook: medium (fine)

Hooking frame

Small scissors

Ironing board and iron

Old towels (2)

Buttonhole twist thread or quilting thread and needle: 1 spool

The wool fabric doesn't need to be 29 inches long. For example, 3 x 29 inches could be 6 x $14^1/_2$ inches or another dimension, as long as you have about 87 square inches (3 x 29 = 87; 6 x $14^1/_2$ = 87).

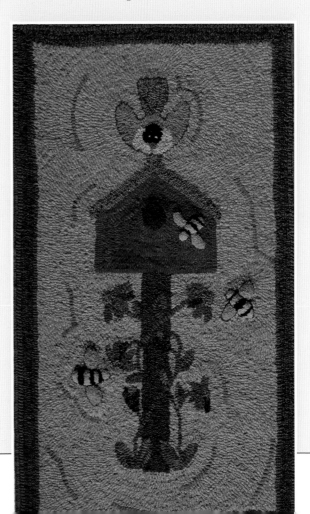

1. Have the pattern enlarged to 32$\frac{1}{2}$ x 19 inches at a copy shop.

2. Leaving a 5-inch border all around, use a pencil and tape measure or yardstick (for measuring) to draw the 32$\frac{1}{2}$ x 19–inch outline of the pattern onto the backing fabric. Be careful to draw along the grain (the direction of the fibers) of the fabric.

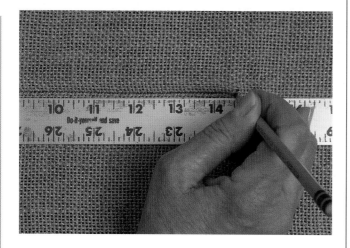

3. Pin the tulle to the pattern.

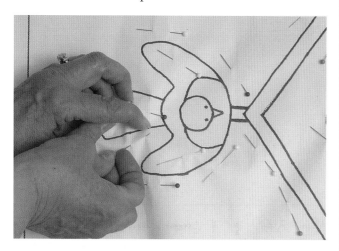

Growing Dimensions

The dimensions of a finished piece may be slightly larger than the pattern, because hooked rugs tend to stretch out a bit and "grow" as they're hooked.

4. With the permanent marker, lightly trace the pattern and outside outline onto the tulle. If the tulle stretches

out of shape too much, add more pins or use a lighter touch.

5. Take out the pins to remove the tulle from the pattern.

6. Line up the straight outside edges of the tulle pattern and the pencil outline on the backing and pin in place.

7. With the permanent marker, trace the pattern onto the backing.

8. Remove the pins to remove the tulle from the backing.

9. To prevent fraying of the edges of the backing fabric while you work, zigzag the raw edges of the backing with a sewing machine.

10. Put the backing on the frame as in chapter 5, steps 9 and 10.

11. When you've selected your wool for hooking, determine the lengthwise grain. (See chapter 3, steps 11 to 14.)

12. Almost all of the strips are #8 cut (¹/₄ inch)—the others are indicated.

13. To cut the #4 cut (¹/₈ inch) strip for the bird's beak, cut an #8 cut strip in half lengthwise, or use a cutting machine with a #4 cutting head.

14. Hook the maroon birdhouse hole by outlining and filling.

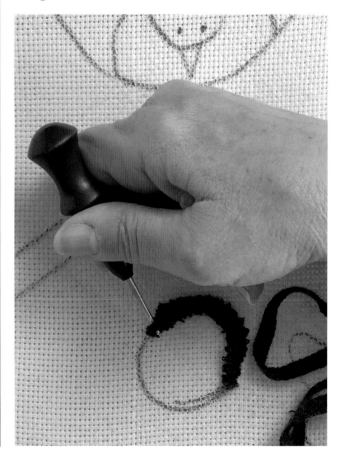

15. The birdhouse roof is hooked in three parallel rows of charcoal herringbone.

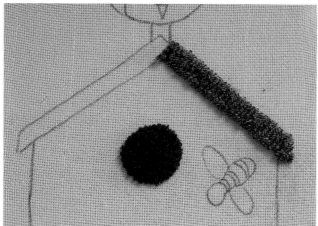

16. If hooking the bees normally, begin by hooking the black stripes (instructions for sculpting the bees begin on page 123).

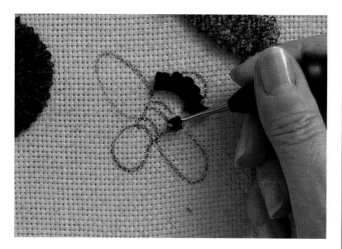

17. Hook with the gold to finish the bees' bodies.

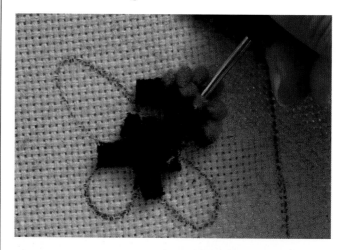

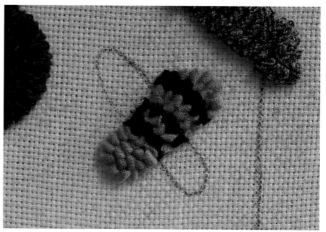

18. Bee wings are hooked in gray by outlining and then filling.

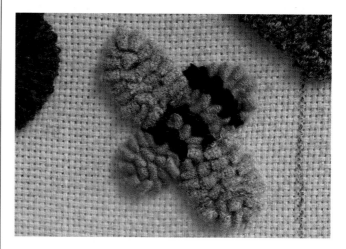

If you're hooking your own design or reproducing a pattern smaller or larger than indicated in the instructions, it's helpful to know how to estimate how much wool you'll need. These are approximate guidelines based on the strip width you're using and the type of hooking you're doing.

- For #8 cut, multiply the area to be covered by 5.
- For sculpting, multiply the area to be covered by 14.

Wool Colors

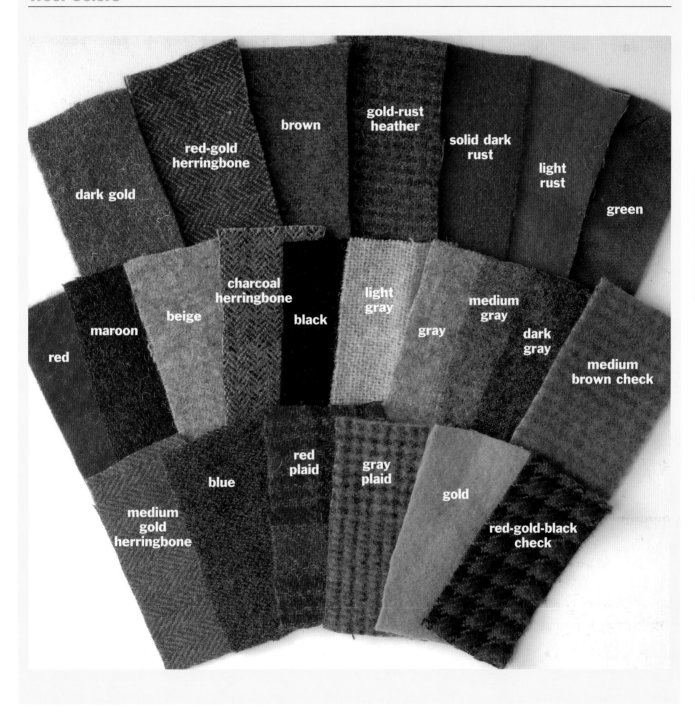

19. To hook the red birdhouse, first outline the house, the bee in front of it, and the hole, then hook along the house outlines in repeated rows until you reach the center, filling in odd shapes around the bee.

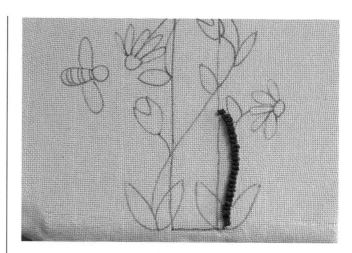

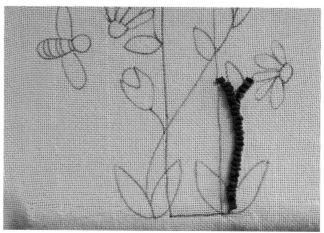

20. Hook the brown vines in a single row on the pattern lines, starting from the bottom up as they would grow.

21. For the flowers, begin by hooking the centers in the same charcoal herringbone used for the roof.

22. Hook each petal in one of the five rust and gold wools, outlining each and filling.

23. For the buds, use red-gold-black check for the outer parts and light rust for the centers.

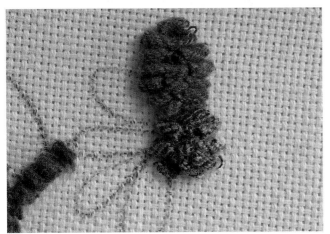

24. Outline and fill the green leaves.

25. For the pole, use blue to outline and fill in vertical rows.

26. Cut a light gray ¹/₄-inch strip in half lengthwise for bird eyes.

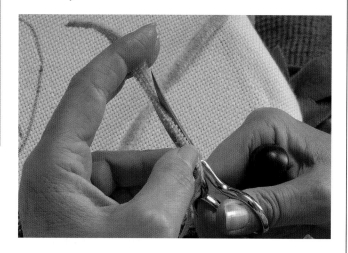

For steps 27 to 33 below, refer to the illustrations in chapter 3, pages 44–46.

27. For bird eyes, pull the end of a ¹/₈-inch strip up through the backing about ¹/₂ inch.

28. Right next to it, hook one loop.

29. Behind the first strip you pulled up, on the other side from the loop, pull up another loop in the same hole you used to pull up the first strip.

30. Cut the last loop in two at its top. With your left hand, pull the remainder of the strip from beneath the backing.

31. Cut off the top of the strip you pulled up first, level with the top of the remaining loop.

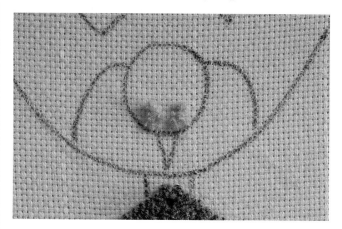

Rules for the Back of the Rug

- Don't be tempted to run a strip across the back to get from one place to another. (See photo on page 29.) This is never done in rug hooking, because a strip of any length across the back, no matter how short, can be snagged and result in pulled-out loops. The strip would also be subject to excess wear.
- There is no knotting in rug hooking. The snugness of the hooking keeps the loops in place. The backing gets tighter as you put in more loops, helping to hold the loops in place.
- Never leave the end of a strip on the back of the rug. Each row of hooking always starts and stops with ends pulled to the top and trimmed level with surrounding loops.

32. Hook the bird's head in black, outlining and filling.

33. The bird's beak is hooked in #4 cut ($^1/_8$ inch) medium gold herringbone. The loops should be $^1/_4$ inch high, the same as the #8 cut loops.

34. Hook the bird's breast in light gray, outlining and filling.

Though most hooked rugs are intended for floors, many people prefer to display them on walls. When hanging a rug, it's important to make sure that its weight is evenly and well supported. To hang a smaller rug such as *Bird and Bees*, follow these steps.

1. Cut a piece of furniture webbing the length of the top edge of the rug.

2. Zigzag the cut ends.

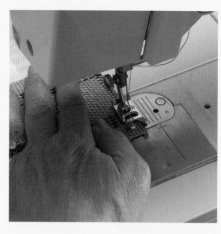

3. Fold the webbing in half lengthwise.

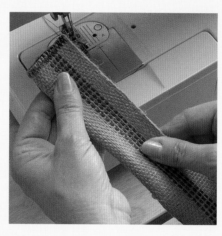

4. Sew the long edges together about ¼ inch from the edge.

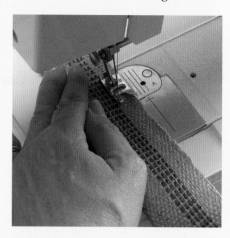

5. With a needle and buttonhole twist or quilting thread, whip the two long edges of the folded webbing to the back of the rug along its top edge, making sure to catch the backing in the needle and not just the bottom of the wool loops.

Whipping stitches can be about ½ inch apart.

6. Cut a piece of wooden lath or lattice slightly shorter than the top edge of the rug and slip it into the casing created by the doubled webbing.

7. On the back of the rug, tack hanging hardware to the encased lath. The rug is now ready for hanging.

8. For large, heavy rugs, use artists' canvas stretchers (page 8) the same dimensions as the rug, and whip the back of the rug to the stretchers.

35. Outline the medium gray bird wings and back and fill.

36. The tail is hooked in gray plaid by outlining and filling.

37. Hook bird legs in two single rows of light rust.

38. To hook the border, begin along one outside edge (not at a corner) with a row of brown. (To make square corners, see the box in chapter 5, page 98.)

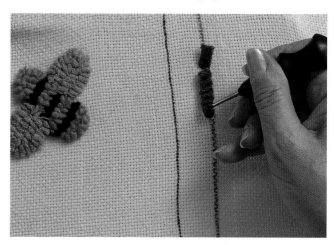

39. Hook three rows of red plaid along and inside the row of brown.

41. Using the background beige, outline the bird, birdhouse, bees, pole, vines, and flowers. Fill in the background by continuing to add rows of outlining. Here and there add some medium brown check to the background. Fill in any odd spaces with the beige.

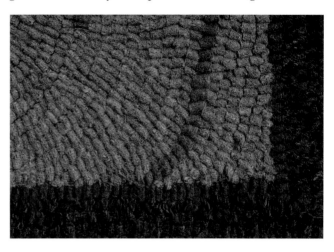

42. If the bird or bees don't contrast well enough with the background fabric you've chosen, outline them with #4 cut ($^1/_8$ inch) dark gray.

40. Finish the border with another row of brown along the inside edge.

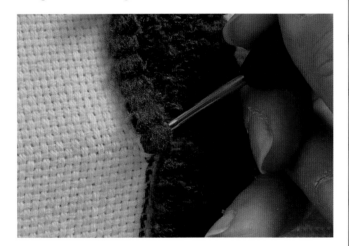

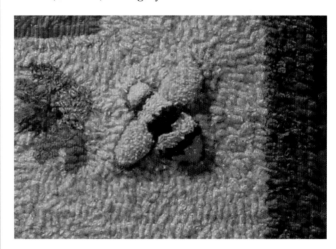

43. After the rug is completely hooked, turn it over to check for any places on the backing that are too sparsely hooked, called "holidays." As the rug wears, these will become obvious bare spaces on the front, so they need to be filled in. See chapter 5, page 98, for instructions on how to fill holidays.

44. Bind the edge the same way as for *Back Home Again* in chapter 5, steps 40 to 54. Instead of using a double strand of one color of yarn as you did in whipping the edge around *Back Home Again*, you might want to use two different colors of yarn, one a little lighter and one a little darker than the brown row hooked along the outer edge of the border, as shown here.

45. Steam the rug to make it lie flat as in chapter 5, steps 55 through 60.

Note: If you have sculpted the bees, do not rest the iron on top of them. Hold the iron slightly above the wet towel to steam the areas where the bees are.

Sculpting Bees

The #3 cut ($^3/_{32}$ inch) wool for sculpting can be cut by machine or by hand. For this very thin strip, be sure to cut along the lengthwise grain of fabric. Fabric quantities for sculpting appear in parentheses on the materials list.

1. Using a "fine" hook (usually marked "F" on the end) and #3 cut ($^3/_{32}$ inch) gold wool, pull up long loops, at least 1 inch high.

2. Hook tightly. There's a special way of doing this that's a little like a running stitch used in embroidery. Begin as usual by pulling up the end of a strip.

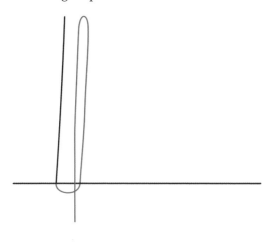

3. Hook a long loop in the next hole.

4. Return to the hole you used for the end of the strip and hook another long loop there.

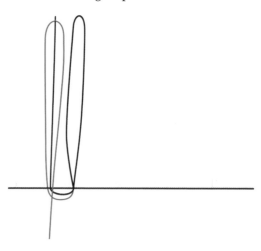

5. Now skip the hole you used to hook the first loop and go one hole beyond it, hooking another long loop.

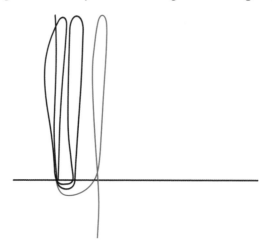

6. Return to the hole you used for the first loop and hook a second loop in it.

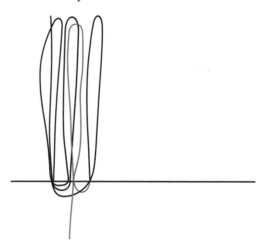

7. Then skip the next hole, which already has a loop in it, to go to the hole after it to hook a loop.

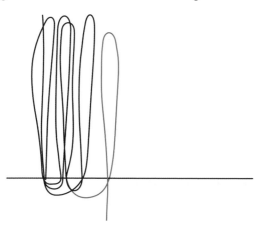

8. Return again to the preceding hole to hook another loop. It's basically two steps forward, one step back. Refer to the diagrams. It sounds more complicated than it is.

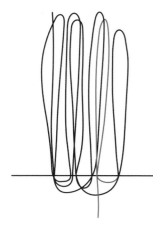

9. After you've hooked the gold and the black stripes, the bee's body will resemble a many-petaled flower. (At this point some hookers prefer to cut the top of each loop so that straight ends stick up instead of loops, but others prefer to skip this step.)

10. Holding the tops of a few loops with one hand, use a small pair of scissors to begin trimming the wool loops, just a little at a time.

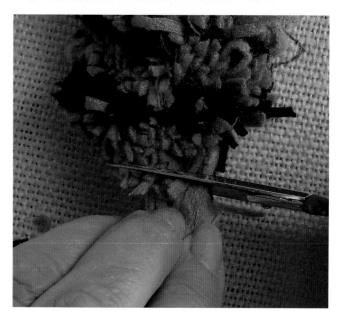

11. Continue trimming a bit at a time, as you slowly achieve the rounded bee shape. At its thickest point, in the middle of the body, the finished bee is about $^3/_4$ inch high, from the backing up.

12. Trim a bit more to reveal the neck.

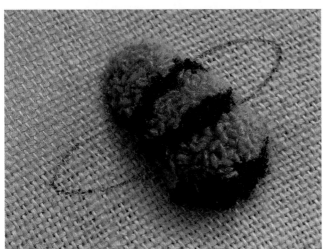

13. Hook and trim the wings the same way.

7

Pedulas: Hooked Whimsies

Pedulas are pure imagination worked in wool. At some unknown point in rug hooking history, the word was assigned to the fanciful flowers that appear on rugs but not in books of horticulture. Pedulas escaped from rugs to appear as lapel pins or in flower pots. Easy and quick to hook and construct, they're a light floral dessert on the rug hooking buffet.

Backing: large enough to fit on a small frame or hoop. You might want to put several pedulas on one piece of backing, leaving at least a 1-inch margin around each.

Bridal tulle (optional): large enough to cover pattern

Wool (any colors)*

Flower (center): 1 12- to 18-inch strip

Flower (petals): $1/2$ x 29 inches (depending on length of loops)

Flower (leaves): $2^1/2$ x 4 inches

Quilter or dressmaker pins

Permanent marker, black

Sewing machine with zigzag (optional) and thread

Masking tape (optional)

Dressmaker shears

Cutting machine with #8 cutting wheel (optional)

Hook: medium or coarse

Embroidery hoop, quilting hoop, or hooking frame

Small scissors

Glue

Pin back

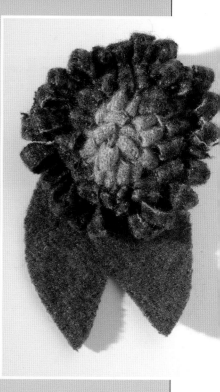

* The wool fabric doesn't need to be 29 inches long. For example, 3 x 29 inches could be 6 x $14^1/2$ inches or another dimension, as long as you have about 87 square inches (3 x 29 = 87; 6 x $14^1/2$ = 87).

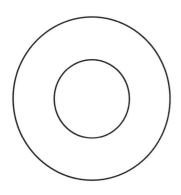

Patterns shown actual size.

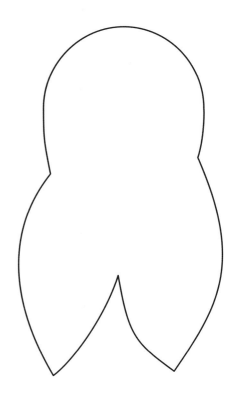

1. Use a piece of backing large enough to fit on your hooking frame or hoop. If desired, plan to hook several flowers on a large piece of backing, leaving at least a 1-inch border around each.

2. Pin the tulle to the pattern. (Or you can draw round flower shapes directly onto the backing.)

3. Using the permanent marker, lightly trace the pattern onto the tulle. If the tulle stretches out of shape too much, use more pins and a lighter touch.

4. Take out the pins to remove the tulle from the pattern.

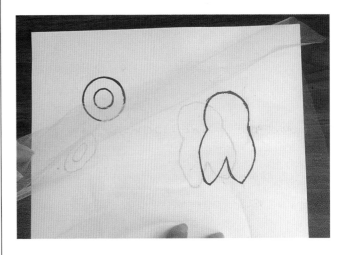

5. Pin the tulle in place over the backing.

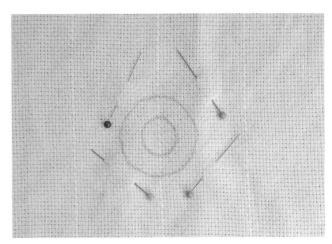

6. With the permanent marker, trace the pattern onto the backing.

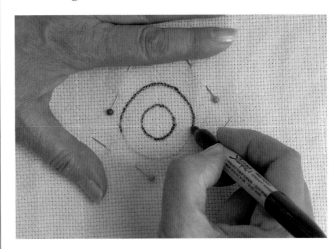

Pedulas

7. Remove the pins to remove the tulle from the backing.

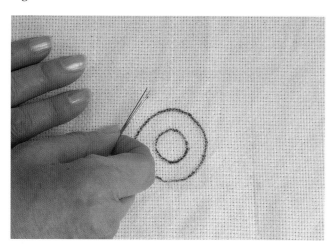

8. Zigzag the raw edges of the backing with a sewing machine to prevent fraying.

9. Put the backing on a frame. An embroidery hoop would work well for these small pieces.

10. Cut wool strips along the grain of the fabric by hand or by machine. These are all #8 cut ($^1/_4$ inch).

Pedula variety

There's no limit to what you can do with a pedula. Try using ribbons instead of wool. Use a stud earring in the center or cut off the clip of a clip earring and sew the earring on with clear thread or glue it in place. Use hot glue to add beads. Use thin strips and wide strips, either long and loopy or short like the center of a sunflower. Plant your woolen garden with varieties that never before saw the light of day.

11. Outline and fill the center in one color.

12. In a contrasting color, begin hooking around the center. With each new row of hooking, make the loops higher.

13. When you get to the outside, the loops can be up to 1¹/₂ inches long.

14. On the back side, spread Aleene's Tacky Glue around the edge of the hooked area to about ¹/₈ inch beyond hooking, working the glue into the backing. Let dry.

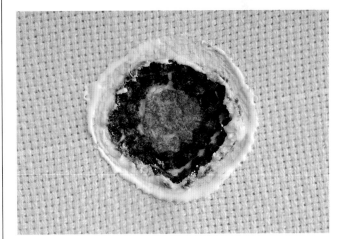

15. Trim the excess backing away, leaving only about ¹/₈ inch near the base of the loops.

16. Pin the leaf pattern to green wool and cut out.

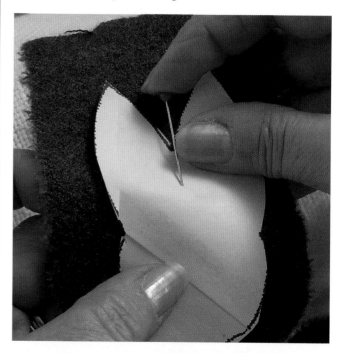

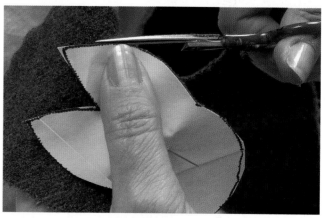

17. Apply glue to the back of the pedula and spread it over the surface.

18. Glue the pedula to the rounded part of the leaf.

19. Turn pedula and leaf right side up and put a small heavy object on top to keep pedula and leaf in contact as glue dries.

20. Glue a pin back to the back of the pedula.

Resources

Association of Traditional Hooking Artists (ATHA), www.atharugs.com. Newsletter, events, classes, resource list of suppliers and teachers by state.

Bee Line Art Tools, P.O. Box 130, Bettendorf, IA 52720, 866-218-1590, www.beelinearttools.com. Bee Line (Townsend) cutter and accessories.

Bolivar, P.O. Box 539, Bridgewater, Nova Scotia, Canada B4V 2X6, 902-543-7762, www.bolivarcutter.com, sales@bolivarcutter.com. Bolivar cutter.

The Dorr Mill Store, P.O. Box 88, Guild, NH 03754, 800-846-3677, www.dorrmillstore.com, dorrmillstore@nhvt.net. Complete line of hooking supplies.

Ebay, www.ebay.com. This internet auction site often has cutters, hooking frames, and other hooking supplies.

Harry M. Fraser Co., 433 Duggins Road, Stoneville, NC 27048, 336-573-9830, www.fraserrug.com, fraserrugs@aol.com. Fraser and Bliss cutters, patterns, complete line of hooking supplies.

Goat Hill Designs, 247 Goat Hill Road, Lambertville, NJ 08530, 609-397-4885, www.goathilldesigns.com, gailduf@aol.com. Complete line of hooking supplies.

Green Mountain Hooked Rugs, 802-223-1333, www.greenmountainhookedrugs.com, info@greenmountainhookedrugs.com. Patterns, backing, fabric, and other supplies.

Gruber's Quilt Shop, 310 4th Avenue NE, Waite Park, MN 56387, 877-778-7793 or 320-259-4360, www.grubersquiltshop.com, sue@grubersquiltshop.com. Lap frames, wool, rug hooking supplies.

Howard Brush, 581 N. Main Street, P.O. Box 1056, Woonsocket, RI 02895, 800-556-7710, www.howardbrush.com, info@howardbrush.com. Gripper strips for hooking frames.

Mayflower Textiles Company, Inc., P.O. Box 329, Franklin, MA 02038, 508-528-3300, www.mayflowertextiles.com, orders@mayflowertextiles.com. Puritan lap frame (metal).

Primitive Spirit, P.O. Box 1363, Eugene, OR 97440, 541-344-4316, www.primitivespiritrugs.com. Patterns.

Rigby Precision Products, 249 Portland Road, P.O. Box 158, Bridgton, ME 04009, 207-647-5679. Rigby cutter.

Rug Hooking Magazine, www.rughookingmagazine.com. Articles and books on rug hooking.

Spruce Ridge Studios, 1786 Eager Road, Howell, MI 48855, 517-546-7732, www.spruceridgestudios.com, kris@spruceridgestudios.com. Patterns and supplies.

W. Cushing & Company, 21 North Street, P.O. Box 351, Kennebunkport, ME 04046, 800-626-7847, www.wcushing.com, customer@wcushing.com. Complete line of hooking supplies.

Whispering Hill Farm, Box 186 Route 169, South Woodstock, CT 0267, 860-928-0162, www.whisperinghill.com, whisperhill@earthlink.net. Verel (polyester) backing and rug hooking supplies.

The Wool Studio, 706 Brownsville Road, Sinking Spring, PA 19608, 610-678-5448, www.thewoolstudio.com. Wool, backing, hooking stands, hooks.

Woolley Fox LLC, 132 Woolley Fox Lane, Ligonier, PA 15658, 724-238-3004, www.woolleyfox.com. Patterns, hooks.

Woolrich, 2 Mill Street, P.O. Box 138, Woolrich, PA 17779, 877-512-7305, www.woolrich.com. Wool fabrics.